⚲ *What do former champions think of* Intelligent Doubles?

"Skip has captured all the fundamentals of the game of doubles which has been both challenging and fun for me to play over the years. After reading this I'm sure you'll learn how to get more out of your own game on the doubles court. I enjoyed reading every chapter!"
— Evonne Goolagong-Cawley, holder of ninety-two international titles and the sole inductee into the Tennis Hall of Fame in 1988.

"For those who wish to enjoy doubles more, this book is a must read. From all the tips contained within, every player should improve their doubles play. Well worth reading!"
— Neale Fraser, Australian Davis Cup Captain the past twenty years and winner of every major doubles title at least once.

"Skip handles all the essentials of playing good doubles so well. This book certainly can heighten one's enjoyment by offering a clear understanding of the game of doubles."
— Virginia Wade, winner of numerous singles and doubles titles throughout her career including five Grand Slam Doubles events. Currently a tennis commentator on ESPN.

"I thoroughly enjoyed reading both *Intelligent Tennis* and *Intelligent Doubles*. Skip has written books which can be very important learning tools for tennis players of all levels. There are many, many good tips in this book, especially on forming and keeping partnerships with regard to both doubles and mixed doubles."
— Owen Davidson, holder of twelve Grand Slam Doubles and Mixed Doubles titles. The only man in history to win the Grand Slam of Mixed Doubles, with partner Billie Jean King.

Intelligent Doubles

A Sensible Approach to Better Doubles Play

Skip Singleton, USPTA Professional

Foreword by Rod Laver

BETTERWAY PUBLICATIONS, INC.
WHITE HALL, VIRGINIA

Published by Betterway Publications, Inc.
P.O. Box 219
Crozet, VA 22932
(804) 823-5661

Cover design by Susan Riley
Cover painting © by LeRoy Neiman
Photographs © Russ Adams Productions, Inc.
Typography by East Coast Typography, Inc.

Library of Congress Cataloging-in-Publication Data

Singleton, Skip
    Intelligent doubles : a sensible approach to better doubles
play / Skip Singleton; foreword by Rod Laver.
        p. cm.
        Includes index.
        ISBN: 1-55870-123-0 : $9.95 (pbk.)
        1. Tennis–Doubles.   2. Tennis — Psychological aspects. I. Title.
GV1002.8S58 1989   796.342'28–dc20   89-36142   CIP

Printed in the United States of America
0 9 8 7 6 5 4 3 2 1

*This book is dedicated to the many teams
I've been fortunate enough to work with.
Thanks for allowing me so much
growth through your teaching.*

*And to my lovely partner in life, Debbie,
who continues to show me ways
to be a better team player.*

ℚ *FOREWORD*

Intelligent Doubles offers a straightforward approach to improving your doubles game. It provides wonderful insight and many good tips on ways to enjoy a better game of doubles at every level, both social and competitive.

Most players identify with the game of doubles but don't practice enough to gain the necessary level of consistency to improve their play. To play this game well requires a great deal of mental preparation and teamwork, along with strategic understanding and consistent stroke making. Although there are no secrets to sound doubles, I feel this is one of the few books available on doubles that you can continue to read and grow from. The checklist under each summary helps to provide you with a quick refresher once you have absorbed each of the chapters in the book.

I've known Skip over the years to be a knowledgeable teacher of the game and respected coach by many. He understands what it takes to become a winning doubles player. His practical style of teaching makes the game easily understood while he covers the mental game, teamwork, shot selection, positioning, and interpersonal relations on the court in a positive and motivating way. This sensible approach to the game of doubles makes for a fine book. I've enjoyed reading it and feel you will as well.

Rod Laver

This book was written to provide positive, motivational, and sensible doubles advice for players of all levels. Another book that I wrote, *Intelligent Tennis,* was written for all players in the sport of tennis with a message which could equally be applied to the game of singles or doubles. *Intelligent Doubles* is, however, *different.* The subject matter of this book pertains specifically to the game of doubles. It addresses the strokes and strategies of the game as well as ways to consistently achieve the best play in yourself and your partner on the doubles court.

At the club level, doubles is probably the most popular form of tennis played today. Although many are playing the game, few really understand and play doubles as the separate game it is. This presents a definite advantage for those who learn more about and come to understand doubles as a unique game. Successful singles players will continue to struggle with the advancement of their doubles play until they recognize the *doubles difference.*

The secret to successful doubles has been thought by some to simply be, "find a great partner"! There is, however, more to this game than pairing with a brilliant player to carry you in the matches you play. A partnership must be developed between two with a common understanding and working relationship. Two minds must be able to come together as one as well as two personalities which show mutual respect and trust for each other on the court. Movement, positioning, shot selection, strategies, and even goals will then be formulated and executed as a pair or more specifically, as a *team.*

To play this game well, players will be required to execute a wider variety of strokes than is normally called for in a game of singles. This book explains the use of these strokes and discusses control of each. It also teaches ways to take control of your opponents, the matches you play, and yourself on the doubles court. It is intended to help you and your partner develop a *mental edge* and a better strategic understanding of the game of doubles in order to bring out your best play . . . *consistently!*

As you read this book, share the material that you've read with your partner so he or she may benefit as well. It would also be a good idea to pass the book along to your partner after you've finished reading it or encourage them to buy a copy. You will both then continue to learn and grow together which is so vitally important in the development of a successful doubles team.

Contents

1. The Doubles Difference 13

2. Developing as a Team 21

3. Playing the Game in Control 35

4. Positioning for Success 47

5. Achieving Consistent Results 71

6. The Midcourt Advantage 81

7. Double(s) Trouble 91

8. Movers, Poachers, and Shakers 103

9. Advancing Through the Levels 115

10. Divorce Court Doubles 129

11. Double the Fun 139

Index 151

CHAPTER 1

The
Doubles Difference

♐ A GAME FOR EVERYONE

"Doubles is really a better game than singles or any other sport you care to mention." Bill Talbert.

Doubles, which is often billed as the "art form of tennis," has been gaining in popularity over the years with players from the beginner ranks all the way to the professionals.

So what's the big attraction? Just what is it about this game of doubles that is inviting so many new players to the game as well as converting many long-time singles enthusiasts?

As a social sport, tennis has always ranked up there among the very best. Golf, bowling, sailing, skiing, and other sports have held their social value; however, because of doubles, tennis continues to be one of the social leaders. With doubles, families can play together (and stay together), friends can pair up, and it's an easy way to make new friends and acquaintances. Let's face it, doubles simply offers more fun than singles. It's less exhausting than a game of singles and is usually more socially played as well. And when four players are involved, the countless variables and happenings on the court can make for one exciting and enjoyable day of tennis for all!

Doubles is also becoming quite popular with tournament players and league participants at all levels. The physical requirements in doubles are usually much less demanding than

13

they are in singles, which opens the door to many competitive souls who might not be able to compete in tennis were it not for the game of doubles. To the older, slower, or heavier set, this may just be the only game in town. But the real beauty of doubles is that two players can come together and form quite a formidable pair no matter what age or weight they are.

In parts of the country where the hot climates prohibit the masses from singles play, doubles matches are more common unless it's very early in the morning or into the evening. And at extremely active clubs and indoor complexes, court time is not only quite expensive, but it can also be difficult to obtain. The solution to both — "let's play doubles!"

It seems that everyone is getting into the act of doubles play. And why not? It can be tennis played at its finest. With the action and excitement in the sport, well-played doubles could even be called the "greatest show on earth"! But is it always? Let's take a look at why the "greatest show on earth" could also be labeled at times, "doubled up singles"!

♀ THE AVERAGE GAME OF DOUBLES

In order to play the game well, an important requirement for a doubles pair is to be able to play *together,* that is, like a *team.* Tennis though, tends to breed individuality among its participants. Shot selection, placement, and execution all are performed uniquely by the players in the game and that's one of the joys of tennis. It brings out the individual skills and talents. However, it also naturally makes people into singles players. Great news for you doubles artists! You see, there are very few tennis players who will ever become really good doubles players. To most, doubles is just an extension of singles play, so the average game of doubles continues to be four players on a doubles court all trying to play singles.

To adapt your singles game to that of a doubles player will require you, first and foremost, to understand that doubles is *not* singles. It is a separate game of tennis which should be played separately. Individual thoughts and actions must learn to give way to the team effort. "For the good of the team" will be your new adopted motto, with "me, myself, and I" taking a back seat while you're on the doubles court. Your individuality may not have to be totally squelched when you form a partnership with another. Good doubles teams take into account the styles of each player when formulating what shots and strategies will be used by the team. The important thing to remember is that the *team* dictates the shots and strategies, not the individual players independently of each other. The best partnerships evolve when two players learn to work together to accomplish a similar task. It is teamwork that brings doubles players the most success, as well as understanding and playing doubles as the separate game it is.

⚲ WHAT MAKES DOUBLES SO DIFFERENT?

Beyond the obvious fact that four participate in doubles while two players go at it in singles play, there are very few similarities in singles and doubles. Oh sure, you still bat a fuzzy yellow tennis ball over a net within some boundary lines just like in singles, however, the boundary lines change and so do the strokes in doubles. The court becomes nine feet wider on either side of the net, thanks to the alleys. While the serve, forehand, and backhand continue to challenge most players in the game, the strokes in doubles offer an even greater challenge to its participants. The addition of strokes such as the lob, volley, half-volley, lob-volley, drop-volley, chip shot, and others makes doubles into a game requiring a much larger arsenal of strokes. This is one of the big reasons why good doubles can be more difficult to play than singles.

Finesse will often beat power in doubles. It is a combination of touch and angles along with consistency, not brute strength and winners, that produces optimum results in doubles. Serves are hit for placement, balls are directed at opponents' feet and put-aways are hit only when in the correct position to attempt such shots. Although some of the most successful professional doubles stars of today are making their mark with "power doubles" play, chances are your best doubles will never consistently come through the use of power. Placement and finesse along with percentage stroke-making are the foundation on which to build your winning doubles game.

Quicker exchanges of the ball occur in doubles as players at the net intercept the ball and place it back to the opponents much sooner than would normally occur in singles. It is these quicker exchanges coupled with finesse and control of well-placed angles that often make doubles a more enjoyable game to play and watch.

The movements of the players in the game of doubles are also very different. In singles, players often move laterally, while in doubles players move more forward and backward. With a partner sharing half the court, there is less need for lateral movement. And as we shall later discuss, good doubles requires movement to the net which gives you the "upward" movement on the court and if the ball is lobbed, the "backward" movement to retreat for it.

With four people sharing the court instead of two, tennis also becomes more complicated. Personalities often differ and when placed under stressful and pressuring situations, anything is possible! Concentration becomes tougher to control in doubles due to the many variables created on the court when more players are present. Since all players are not involved in every hit on their side of the court, it is possible for their minds to wander. Players who prefer to keep quiet and to themselves while playing tennis might find it hard to adjust to communicating on the doubles court while keeping their concentration sharp.

Strategies in singles and doubles matches are also quite different and varied. Singles play usually requires strategic planning to take into account several variables such as the opponents' game, the playing surface, and the limitations of the players involved. Doubles players on the other hand have more variables to contend with. Although court surface speed doesn't play as important a role in forming a doubles strategy, by increasing the number of participants to four, the variables increase dramatically. The strengths and weaknesses of all four players must be taken into account as well as the strengths and weaknesses of each team. Doubles strategies must also be more flexible since changes are more likely to occur in doubles.

⚲ IS DOUBLES THE GAME FOR YOU?

So what do you think . . . is this game of doubles really the right game for you?

Psychologists and psychiatrists who have studied tennis players have found that doubles players are better liked than singles players. They have discovered that teamwork makes for better interpersonal relations, and that the players in doubles are thus easier to get along with.

Singles players often have difficulty sharing the court and the responsibility for doubles play. "Court hog" is a favorite term used to describe singles players who lack an understanding of doubles play. They dart about the court oblivious to any or all team efforts. These same individuals may also have a difficult time sharing the credit or blame for the team's wins or losses. They are often selfish people and won't become true doubles players until they learn to shed their "me, me" attitude and become a *team* with their partner.

One of the toughest things to swallow is that being a good singles player will not necessarily make you a good doubles player. And if you're a hotshot singles player, you might even be considered a misfit on the doubles court! Ouch. That can be hard to accept.

So what is all this leading up to? If you really want to learn to play your best doubles you must first understand that *doubles* is a separate game than singles and must be played *separately*. Once you commit yourself to understanding and applying this fact along with the principles discussed in this book, you'll be on your way to playing intelligent doubles. If you continue to think and act only for yourself on a doubles court, your successes will be few. However, if you learn to work together with another, there will be limitless possibilities of fun and exercise for you both.

♀ WHY SHOULD I WANT TO BE A SECOND CLASS CITIZEN?

The singles players in the game of tennis get all the glory. They are the center court stars who will get most of the attention and admiration from the public. They are the famous ones in the game because they are in the limelight. What then are the doubles players of the game? Sorry for the bad news, folks, but at least for now, you may find yourself treated like a second class citizen for taking up the game of doubles.

Even at the professional level, doubles is often played late in the evening or at irregular hours and is usually played on side or back courts leaving the prime time and prime courts for you know who . . . those "singles stars"! The crowds and the television cameras might also be long gone by the time the doubles teams even take to the courts. Some of the best professional tennis is rarely ever seen because it's being played on the doubles court.

Why do singles players get all the star treatment and not the doubles players? With the pros, money might have something to do with it. Singles champions receive about seven times the prize money of each member of the winning doubles team. Superstar singles players also draw the big crowds to the tournaments and to the television sets. The press gets hold of them and plugs and plays on their every move until it draws the public attention. What has been a great boost for doubles is when players like John McEnroe, Boris Becker, Steffi Graf, and Martina Navratilova take to the doubles court after their singles play and bring the crowds with them.

I can hear the doubles players screaming, "I get no respect!", and rightly so. Doubles is a great game; many even consider it to be the greatest. Why then should you want to be a second class citizen? Why play doubles when you could gain superstar status as a singles player? Whoa . . . wait just a minute. Playing singles will not necessarily make you into a superstar. There will only be one winner in every singles tournament played with everyone else losing out. You will find that there are really very few superstars in tennis at any level you play the game. Tennis will be played as a game of enjoyment for the rest. Winning can bring enjoyment in both singles and doubles, however, *some* of the greatest enjoyment you will ever get out of tennis can be had on a doubles court with the right *partner*. It might not even come from winning but rather from improving together and learning to play your best doubles . . . consistently! It is a terrific feeling to be able to understand the game of doubles, share it with another, and then develop and improve together. In any case, the enjoyment you will derive from doubles play will surely overshadow your citizenship status!

ℚ *SEARCHING FOR THE RIGHT (OR LEFT) PARTNER*

Now comes the time for you to search out and find that special someone with whom you will share your court. But before you go out looking for Mr. or Ms. Right, there are a few important points you will need to recognize. You should not necessarily be looking for a person who is identical to you in terms of your play (shots, strength, and quickness), or even matches your taste and personality. The best possible partner to find is one who is both *complementary* and *complimentary.*

The right partner could be a friend you already have; although not a necessary requirement, it often helps. It should be someone, however, with whom you are compatible, get along with, and can talk to easily. You should also keep in mind when searching for a partner that you're looking for a "team player." Flashy individuals can be impulsive, self centered, and quite difficult to pair up with. Even though they might have brilliant moments and look impressive at times, forming lasting relationships with these players can prove disastrous in the long run.

If you find someone willing to share the credit or blame with you for winning or losing, you will find an individual with whom you will share mutual respect and confidence. The last thing you want to feel is embarrassment or guilt after missing each shot, and it will be your partner (and the relationship that you have) who will either make you feel that way or not. It will take a mutually supportive balance to keep the level of confidence riding high for you both. *Forgiveness, support,* and *understanding* are the foundation for building a bond of respect. Look for someone with whom you can share these important qualities.

Be thinking about how your styles of play would match up. Would this person complement your strengths and weaknesses and would you complement hers? Are both of you leaders or followers, or preferably one of each? Do you play at a similar level? Do you have similar desires and goals for the game?

In searching for a complementary style, know which side of the court (forehand/right/deuce or backhand/left/ad) you prefer to play and look for a partner who plays the other side well. The great doubles teams in the past have had the power player on the left or ad side with the finesse or steady player on the right side. The consistent player on the right will be able to play more balls, as the person who plays this side of the court will have at least as many opportunities if not more to put the ball into play. The player on the ad side will be the opportunistic shot maker who can rise to the occasion on big points and "make it happen." If you're an "ad court" type of player yourself, stay away from pairing up with other ad players unless you want inconsistent results. On the other hand, if you're a steady right side player and team up with another "Steady Eddie" you might find that as a team you lack the "knockout punch" needed to win some points. Search for the right (or left) player who will complement your team and help to unify your efforts.

♀ SUMMARY

When played well, doubles can be the greatest game there is! Few tennis players will ever become really good doubles players because they'll continue to play singles on the doubles court. Doubles is really quite different than singles and should be played that way. From the number of players to the court size, from the shots played to the movement, from the strategies to the required teamwork, doubles has its own special qualities. If you have difficulty sharing the court or the responsibility for doubles play, you might want to consider playing singles instead. However, if you understand the game of doubles and are willing to learn and work with another, great successes await you.

Even though singles will continue (at least for now) to produce the superstars, doubles players around the world will be gaining so much enjoyment from the game that the star status will seem insignificant. The best partner you will ever find will not only complement your style of play but will also be a complimentary type of person.

CHAPTER 2

Developing as a Team

⚘ KNOW THYSELVES

Now you're ready to prove yourselves as a team, a pair that meshes together and wins as one. But before you begin formulating the plans and strategies of your new team, take a good look at yourselves and the games that you play. Without a thorough understanding of each other, how will you ever be able to set and plan strategies for the team to follow? You must first know your capabilities before your team will be ready to set its intentions in motion.

You hope you have chosen a partner who complements your game. Now let's make certain that he is positioned on the side of the court which proves most advantageous. Two right-handers usually find they work best with the better forehand player on the right side and the player with the best backhand on the left. Left-handers usually do more damage to an opposing team from the ad side of the court as well, because their backhands appear almost hidden and make it difficult for servers to find. Although these are generally agreed-upon formations, each team is unique and must be analyzed to discover where the players' strengths and weaknesses lie to determine where each should be positioned for the good of the team.

Players with delusions of grandeur often view themselves as being able to produce any and all shots in the book. Even though these same players often appear confident on the outside, inside their confidence and esteem levels are generally

21

After losing the first set in a tie-breaker, Martina Navratilova and Pam Shriver discuss changes in strategy.

quite low. This is because they have never discovered their own game, so they don't know how to play within it. You must be able to set strategies and game plans that suit your own game and style of play to expect any amount of success in playing them. Don't imagine that you're some player you're not. Try instead to be the person you *are*, understand who that person is and then plan and play your game as that person. Nothing will bring you more consistent results than simply *understanding* your game and playing within *it*.

℺ TWO HEADS ARE BETTER . . .

In doubles, two heads aren't only more convenient, they're essential! Without a "meeting of the minds" players may plan and play *independently* of each other. Strategies, shot selections, opponent evaluations, and other such tactical planning can only be discussed and decided on as a *team*. Any other way would simply be playing separate games of tennis as a tandem.

With two persons pooling their resources, what each person sees, hears, feels, and thinks should be shared to strengthen the overall awareness of the team. What you gain from another point of view can also prove enlightening and even help to sharpen your individual awareness. With two persons across the net from you, there are many more variables to consider. You might pick out something one of the players is doing while your partner picks up on another important occurrence from the opposing team. When each of you shares your findings with the other, not only does the team benefit from your combined discoveries, but you will each improve in your perceptions.

The most complex computer in the world lies in your head. When turned on and focused properly, the possibilities of what you could accomplish mentally are limitless. What happens quite often though, is that many will leave their minds dormant or turned to the "off" position. When two minds come together and join forces, the combined mental outlook of each is that much more enhanced. And it is this united mental effort that will bring the team the sharpest awareness and the most successes.

Pam Shriver and Martina Navratilova ease a tense moment with a little humor.

⚲ THE ART OF COMMUNICATION

The very essence of teamwork begins when a common understanding is firmly established between the partners. This can take the form of several modes of communication, both verbal and nonverbal. Brief "pow-wow" sessions, which occur when teammates meet to share and discuss ideas, are one of the basic as well as most important means of communication in doubles. Strategies might be discussed in these quickie chats or they can even be used as a form of "pep talk" to keep the team both motivated and focused on what is happening.

Players often share what shots they are about to hit or where they will direct the next ball. Why? So their partner will then know what to prepare for. There will be no surprises this way. When a server indicates to the net-playing partner that the serve will be placed out wide, it gives that person at the net a clue that she must be prepared to cover her alley a little more than normal since a serve out wide creates an angle for the receiver conducive to alley placements. Without prior knowledge, the net person might have been a little more relaxed on her alley coverage and been easily passed. Likewise, receivers who are about to hit a lob return would often have more success if they would warn their partner in advance so she will react more quickly if the lob pulls up short and she's faced with a "fuzzy sandwich" coming her way. These in-between-point communications are often helpful and will improve team planning and positioning.

Signaling offers another means of doubles communication. It is most often used by the net person who shows a hidden hand signal behind the back to the server. It lets the server know if he will be "poaching" or moving across the court to intercept the volley or that he should stay put. He might also be indicating to the server where the ball should be directed (left or right) in the service box so he will be in position to react to the return of service. A closed hand could mean "go" while an open hand means "stay." The index finger pointed to the left means serve there, and the thumb showing in the opposite direction indicates the serve should be directed to the right side of the box. If the server has the control, this can be an excellent way for two to work together.

As important as communication is in doubles, too much

can cause concentration failure as more emphasis is placed on sharing thoughts with your partner than on the actual play. For this reason, you and your partner must decide just how much communication is necessary for your team. You might elect to keep your on-court talk to a minimum.

Remember that silence is often golden. If everything is working well and your team is on the right track, the best idea might be just to be quiet and play! You could discover that biting your tongue when you would prefer to talk could benefit you both. Search for the right proportion of communication vs. silence for your team's greatest level of success.

Whether you are the leader or the follower on your team, to be a good communicator requires a talent for *listening*. Those who talk less learn more and hear more! You all know someone who talks so much that he listens to no one. Even as you speak, you can see that he really isn't listening because he is thinking only about what he will say next. This is why the best conversationalists in life, those regarded as the best communicators, are great listeners! When your partner does talk, listen and *learn*.

The most important form of communication you will share with your partner (as well as with your opponents) is the expression on your face. It will tell the whole story of what you're feeling if you don't watch out. Learn to control its action to set the tone for your team. A smile or calm look on your face exudes confidence and can relax your partner more than most words can. A friendly, soothing, or warm look from a partner helps to let your defenses down also, and you might find yourself more willing to listen and perform for her.

⚲ THE DOUBLES DIPLOMAT

Good communication skills require a working knowledge of human relations. It's not always *what* you say in doubles that is important but also *how* you say it. If said wrong, your shared information, no matter how significant, might not be accepted or even received by your partner. People tend to hear what they want to hear, so you must make sure that your partner *wants* to hear what you have to say. How you present your message can even be deemed a "sales pitch." It must be carefully presented especially during stressful and trying times like those during doubles play, and especially when the subject matter is of a personal nature — like his tennis play!

The bottom line for all communications in doubles must be: *Don't get your partner mad or upset.* No one likes to get mad and certainly better play won't be the result. No matter how poorly your partner might be playing remember that they, like you, are playing the best they can that day. Be understanding instead . . . you will experience "off" days also and you will expect their sympathy when your own play is not up to par. Stay away from sarcastic remarks, dirty looks, or using the cold shoulder to your partner. Instead, try to win him over to your side with tact and finesse. By doing so, you will not only score points with your partner, but you'll also probably score more points against your opponents as well.

No one enjoys being on the receiving end of orders. *Questions* offer a tactful way to bring your partner over to your way of thinking. "Do you think our lobbing strategy is the right one to use against this team?" "What do you think we should be doing instead?" This approach always gets better results than simply saying "I wish you'd stop lobbing so much and start hitting the ball!"

Another positive approach is to use "we" in place of "you" when talking with your partner. "We should be doing . . ." sounds more pleasant than "you should be doing . . ." It's not quite as harsh a tactic, places less blame on the individual involved, and puts the task on the team instead. The individual players then want to rally for the team effort and are willing to adopt the team's new course of action. However, when told they themselves must change because of something they're doing, defenses will rise and their confidence will usually lower. Communication then becomes a team destroyer instead of a means of enhancing the success of the team.

Strive to make team talks encouraging and motivating by stating or implying that the needed change is an *easy* task. When thoughts and words of despair enter into the picture, discouragement sets in and brings the team down. A sense of humor never hurts either! When you both can step back and poke fun or joke during special times when the tension is building, it could relax you and bring you closer together. Do be careful of the *tone* you use. It could affect your partner's reaction to your message either positively or negatively.

An important part of understanding people and learning to become a diplomatic doubles player is knowing that people generally like to be made to feel important. Remember also that everyone's own problems are their biggest concerns. These concepts are of utmost importance in communicating with your partner. Communication is a two-way street and you'll need to recognize your partner's feelings when interacting. Take a genuine interest in your partner. Listen with a caring ear, not only to what he says but also to what he must be feeling. Those players who take no interest in others will have great difficulties in doubles and in the game of life!

♀ LET'S FACE IT, IT'S LIKE A MARRIAGE

A doubles team must be built on mutual trust, respect, understanding, communication, and support. Sound familiar? "Do you _____ take thee _____ to be your doubles partner, to have and to play with until losses do you part?"

Just as with a marriage or any other relationship, in doubles you get back what you put in. It might require a little work to keep the team flowing smoothly together. Doubles definitely offers a give-and-take situation, and there are times you must be prepared to do just that, a little more "giving." The "taking" comes from what you will get back through all of your giving. Learn to give without any expectations of receiving and you will certainly gain from it. However, if you're only willing to give conditionally, don't expect to get much back either. After all, you weren't willing to give very much of yourself.

Sensitive and sympathetic support of your partner sends the message of your care and feelings toward him. If you learn to make him feel good about himself through your support, chances are he will play better (for you). You will make him feel relaxed and confident and more willing to work with you as a partner. On the other hand, if you lack the sensitivity to care about your partner after he's missed the last three forehands, don't look for him to rally around and support your next brilliant strategic idea for the team either.

It has been said that love means never having to say you're sorry. Emphatic and repeated apologies should be avoided on the doubles court also. Try to forget about past errors. When you apologize you are only reminding yourself, your partner, and your opponents of your mistakes. Don't dwell on the negative. Instead, try to learn from your errors so you won't repeat them, and then offer encouraging words to yourself and your partner. Go forward in your thoughts and actions and stay away from backward progressions.

Many marriages break down through lack of communication. Make sure that as a doubles pair you are both open to discussions about your team on and off the court (preferably off). This "open door" policy keeps a steady flow of communication possible to avoid built-up negative thoughts. It will take a commitment on your part to establish a strong relationship with your doubles partner. However, once you've decided to work at it and make it a priority, you and your doubles partner might find yourselves successfully together "till death do you part"!

♗ MINE, YOURS, WHOSE?

Learning to play as a team requires an implicit understanding of who will take and play each shot on your side of the court. With most balls it's quite obvious who will return the shot when the players are in the proper formation, however, as you probably realize, there are exceptions to the rule.

The two most common situations of indecision occur when the ball is directed between the two of you down the center of the court and when the ball is played high over your head (or your partner's head). Balls hit down the center of the court should be taken by the strongest player on the team, that is, the better of the two. This can be further defined by which of you has the best stroke down the center of the court. Usually it's the forehand stroke but not always. This is why the team should understand in advance and decide who will play these balls to avoid confusion during actual play. Another consideration might be who played the last shot. If the same person hits the ball again he probably has a better rhythm, is more apt to be ready, and may be a little quicker with his reflexes than his partner.

Which player is closest to the net on balls in question? *The player closest to the net should always be afforded the right of way.* Being closer to the net, this player is positioned better to use the angles created to the team's advantage. She is in a better location to put the ball away and win the point than her partner.

All balls lobbed up overhead to your side of the court should quickly be called out loud with either a "Mine!" or

Circuit veterans Marty Reissen and Sherwood Stewart get caught "clashing rackets", often the result of clever down the center hits.

"Yours!" It is important that this be decided and stated *immediately*, so your partner will know your intentions and be able to prepare and position accordingly. When "mine" is said, you have indicated that you will take the ball so your partner prepares to cover his side of the court. (He should, however, be prepared also to back you up if your judgment is off and you're unable to play the shot.) When "yours" is immediately yelled, you are letting your partner know that you can't get to the ball and you need help. Problems occur with covering lobs when players neglect to call the shot or if the players hesitate too long and make the call late. Players are then left unsure of who will take the ball and chaos results.

"Let it bounce!" and "Switch!" are two other commands that can help the team. "Let it bounce" is quickly called by an alert player to his partner about to strike a ball that appears to be traveling out. And "switch" is the word used to describe what your partner should do after you've crossed over to his side of the court.

⚲ LEARNING TO PLAY AS ONE

Even though everyone has individual tasks in doubles, it is those players who learn to work toward a common cause who will discover the true essence of teamwork and the success that it will bring.

Playing as one is the very basis of good team play. Once you understand your own games, have taken into account the games of your opponents, have come together and communicated a strategy, it will then be important to carry out the mission as *one*. What is often the case is that a doubles team formulates a general strategy prior to the start of the match and then plays the match "impromptu." Very little on-court communication will ensue because very little teamwork is present to begin with. What the team needs first is to get more specific with their strategic planning. Each team member must know what direction the team is heading in order to play his game in the same direction. Without a clear path to follow, players will surely play a game independent of their partner. If the two of you were taking a long trip together in separate cars, you would never consider taking off before sharing your exact course. If only general directions such as "head east" were given, do you think the two of you would end up at the same destination?!

For a doubles pair to continue to play as one, on-court communication must be practiced so the team will be able to adapt or change their plans to allow for the many situations bound to crop up. A team that neglects to stay abreast of these changes can find themselves lagging behind with a strategy that has failed to keep up.

In other sports, players working together as one unit are commonplace. In football the quarterback and center must properly connect with the hike of the ball; in basketball the shooter is useless without the help of the assist man or passer; and in baseball the pitcher and catcher work closely to out-guess the batter. In tennis each doubles pair must also become one. When the team is serving, the net player offers to poach more or advises where to serve when the team gets into trouble. The players aren't silent, they're always working together to try to hold serve as a team. And as the receiving team, they must work even harder to overcome the serving team's offensive advantage.

⚲ IT TAKES TWO TO WIN (OR LOSE!)

The most important thing to remember when developing with your partner into a team is: "You are not playing against your partner." Learn to work *with* your partner, not against her. Everyone has good and bad or hot and cold days, so be understanding and compassionate if your partner's game goes awry. She will never perform at a higher standard if you humiliate her. However, when respect is shown, even at the lowest of moments, your praises will help to restore your partner's needed confidence thereby helping her performance.

Some players do play against their partners. They sometimes get so furious they won't even talk to their teammate for days after playing a so-called "friendly" game of doubles with them. They tend to blame the other instead of accepting equal responsibility for losses. They feel that by isolating their partner they will be signaling to others who actually lost the match for the team. A big ego in one or both of the players can spoil a doubles team faster than you can say, "Anyone for a game of doubles?"

Your confidence, image, and belief in yourself have so much to do with the actions and support your partner shows toward you. He can make you feel good or bad about yourself (and play that way too), and at the same time you have an impact on how your partner feels about himself. Since neither of you can win without the other, learn to show your partner the respect and support you crave from him.

When two players are of mixed levels the stronger player, who often assumes the duties of captain of the team, should take great caution to give only *suggestions* for the team to follow. The weaker player already feels a sense of inadequacy, and instructions for the team must be kept minimal and diplomatic. Care should also be given to expressions and gestures made on the court. No matter how slight, they can prove quite damaging to the self esteem of most players. Sensitivity and responsibility to your partner will be what builds you stronger as one. Remember, you will win or lose every game as a pair, so learn to work and play like one.

ℚ *SUMMARY*

Take a good look at both of your game styles and shot-making abilities before you start making a strategy for the team to follow. Planning and playing within yourselves will bring your team the most consistent results. Put your minds together and share in your thoughts. Not only will you each gain more knowledge, but the team will greatly benefit from your combined observations. Communication is vitally important to keep a pair playing with a common understanding. Search for the best means and ways as well as the correct amount of communication necessary for your team to operate most effectively. It's not always *what* you say but *how* you say it that matters most. Be very diplomatic in your approach with your partner to bring out her very best play. A doubles team could be compared to a marriage. It presents a give-and-take relationship between two, and you will usually get back what you put into it.

Communication with your partner on questionable balls should be made loudly and decisively to keep clear who will play the ball. To be able to "play as one" will require specific plans for the team to follow. Generalizations will surely cause the team to play a separate game of tennis. Since you're not playing against your partner, develop a sensitivity for them to help them rebound from poor play. Accept the responsibility that you will win or lose as a team, so drop the ego, and work with your partner on both his good and bad days.

CHAPTER 3

Playing the Game in Control

♉ GAINING CONTROL OF YOURSELVES

Ohhhh . . . the *power* of being in control. Politicians relish it, business leaders crave it, and many individuals want badly to have it. Being in control can bring with it a sense of command. It is an authoritative "in charge" feeling that brings to so many the joy, luxury, and power of controlling.

Tennis players in search of advancement in the game should take a few notes from successful leaders in the "real world." Being in control does have definite advantages. Tennis players in control of themselves, their minds, and the ball will surely be in control of their opponents and the match as they play. However, without control of yourself or the focus of your mind, your ability to control the ball will be greatly diminished. This hindrance undoubtedly alters your control of your opponent and ultimately your grasp of the match.

Control of yourselves is best described in the single word "discipline." It is this constant regulation over your thoughts and actions which produces the desired "self" you aspire to be. Quite simply, people are seen either "in control" of themselves on the court or "out of control." Most unsportsmanlike conduct can be traced directly to an individual lacking self discipline or self control. These people don't have command of themselves so they will only rarely be consistently in command of the matches they play.

To play your desired game of tennis will require you to be in control of the many situations likely to occur in a match such as changing weather or court conditions, difficult opponents, spectator pressures, or other surrounding nuisances. Players who lack the control of themselves will often let these situations control them by allowing them to distort their play. This is the prime "excuse time" as it's always easier to lay the blame on external happenings than to hold yourself accountable for poor play. Mentally tough competitors, on the other hand, won't be affected by situational factors as they let them bounce off their tough exterior shell and play havoc on their opponents instead. The rhythm and timing of players in control is also quite a contrast to those rushing hurriedly about the court. Smooth flowing strides and strokes are the earmarks of controlled tennis players.

Playing in control means responsible actions. If you find yourself later repeatedly feeling remorseful about your on-court antics and actions, it's time to recognize your deficiency in the self-control department. You can change by simply exercising more discipline over yourself. Stop looking for excuses for your play. Learn to take full responsibility for it. Only *you* are in control of your play, so stop looking for answers elsewhere!

⚲ FOCUSING YOUR MINDS ON THE TASK

Players who exercise their brains on the court by worrying about a stroke or problem they're having won't realize much success in tennis. While the mind must be disciplined about what to think about, it must also be trained to remain focused on the task at hand. A wandering mind will focus nowhere and prove detrimental to play, while a focused one is not only beneficial to play, it is absolutely essential for optimum results.

"Hit and see" tennis is the game many players are familiar with. They simply knock the ball over the net to see what will happen! Very little use of the brain is required to play such a game. Even though the mind isn't working in these players' favor, it is usually quite heavily taxed as the players moan, complain, and sulk about their sub-par performances. More likely than not, these same players just aren't aware of how to use their minds properly in tennis. They are so accustomed to using them for worry, anger, and disgust that they've forgotten that they can be used for benefits as well. They need to discover that it's intelligence that makes winners in tennis. They should use their minds to foster thoughts that are beneficial and not those that are self defeating.

Controlled thinking is what often separates the levels of players. It also decides the way most matches will go. Win the first set, relax your focus, and watch the match slowly slip away. Relax your focus after breaking your opponent's serve and holding your own serve will become a much more difficult struggle. Think on what you did last night or on some important happening in your life, and forget it! Your mind takes you elsewhere and your control over the match is gone. *Concentration* is the art of remaining focused on the here and now. It is blocking out past and future thoughts that can hinder your play. Concentrated players usually won't let mistakes bother them either, because they're in such control of their thoughts that they don't allow negative or self-defeating thoughts to enter and take control.

Being able to stay concentrated with a focused mind is something most players struggle with all of their tennis-playing years. They play well when their minds are "in tune" and erratically when they are not. But how often will these same players attempt to better understand or work harder to develop a greater level of concentration within themselves? Sad to say, it is rare. Most players seem content to scream "watch the ball" to themselves, demanding instant concentration when they miss the easy ones. If only they would learn to *relax* more, clear their minds of all irrelevant thoughts, and discipline their thinking, the focus of their mind could alone heighten their level of play. They might even discover that they wouldn't need to scream "watch the ball" any longer, because they'd already be focused on it. Demanding that you have instant concentration on the court is almost as difficult as demanding that you immediately run a marathon. Neither can be accomplished without proper and thorough preparation, discipline, and desire. You must really want to reach a heightened level of concentration to channel all of your thoughts and energies to the task. It also won't come when *forced.* Relax when you want your concentration level to improve. Once you've learned to master your concentration, you'll discover that its control will be your greatest ally on the court. However, ignore its power and you're destined to labor long and hard to advance your tennis game.

♀ UNDERSTANDING AND EXECUTING BALL CONTROL

Playing the game in control is quite impossible without first understanding and being able to execute control of the ball. Although it's universally understood that tennis balls travel in the direction they are stroked, control of the ball continues to plague most people. The only four mistakes in tennis are: hitting the ball into the net, hitting the ball too long, hitting it too far to the left, and hitting it too far to the right. These four simple mistakes keep teaching professionals around the world in business, as students of the game continue to search for an understanding of how to better control the balls they hit.

Clearly, all mechanics of each stroke occur simply to make proper contact with the ball and to send it in the desired direction. Tennis gurus and other instructional experts love to complicate the stroking process by touting "1,001 proven ways for a better swing." Players then try to incorporate this advice into their own games by altering or changing some part of their stroke, never really understanding how it relates to their control of the ball. They might change a grip, alter their swing, or even move their feet differently thinking this is the answer they've been searching for. Maybe it is, and then again, maybe it isn't. Without the clear understanding of how the change relates to their control of the ball, the change will usually prove useless.

Footwork lines your body up for the required hit, while *racket preparation* gets your racket into position for the desired contact. Your *grip* holds the racket at the proper angle while the firmness of your grip stabilizes the racket's movement throughout the hit for better control. Balls should be played out in front of the body on all hits and taken at a comfortable height and distance away from the body to avoid unnecessary cramping and excessive reaching. Balance of the body is also an important requirement to direct the ball with proper control.

Each of these relates to the other in the stroking process at the *contact point*. This is when the racket face (strings) and ball meet, and it ultimately dictates in which direction the ball will continue to travel. The stroke further progresses with the *follow-through* as the racket continues to swing after contact in the direction of its intended target and directs the ball there in the process.

When mistakes or problems occur with your strokes, look to your contact of the ball. This is where you will usually discover why the ball went in the unwanted direction that it did. "Freeze" at the end of hits for a brief moment to analyze your balance, follow-through, and positioning on your hits. Freeze also when your opponent hits a shot into the net to analyze your racket and body preparation as well as your intensity prior to shots you are preparing to strike. Both of these freeze maneuvers can help you gain valuable insight into your game and a better understanding of your control of the ball.

Sheer power pays off in doubles only when control is present. This is one of the biggest obstacles in successful play, regulating the amount of power so that it comes *with* control. Cannonball serves should be saved for change of pace strategies, while a ¾ speed service with good depth and placement is ideal. Every shot is hit with a target in mind so deliberate *placement* is the key at every level played. Strive to use a controlled swing to hit a controlled ball. Smooth efficient swings that effectively travel through the ball will bring your team the results you desire.

♀ POSITIVE THOUGHTS ONLY, PLEASE

To play the game of doubles in control necessitates gaining command of your thoughts. Anyone who allows thoughts of despair, doubt, or hopelessness to enter his mind will wallow in his own pessimism. Teams in control of their thoughts will funnel words of encouragement to themselves, which in turn fuel powerful optimism. The strength of selective positive thinking is quite remarkable. You are what you think, so train yourself to think like a winner!

Errors and poor play are what generally test the strength of one's mental armor. It's easy to show dissatisfaction with mistakes; however, it shows character and mental toughness to be emotionally unaffected by them. Errors should be quickly forgotten after corrective analysis as players remember instead the good shots they've been playing. How many times have you played a game of doubles and after hitting ten to fifteen good shots remember only the bad mistakes you made earlier? What about the shots your partner hit? Do you keep remembering the several mistakes she made, or do you remain positive by choosing instead to focus on her better play? You are in control of your thinking and have the choice between thoughts that put you and your partner down or pick you and your partner up.

In doubles, thoughts of *guilt* are often the biggest reason some will choose playing singles over doubles. "I don't want to let my partner down" is a common reaction by many who fear poor play. They put such pressure on themselves to perform at a superhuman level without mistakes that they become predetermined "negative thinkers." While some singles players trying to play doubles do apply the pressures of guilt on their partner, often these feelings simply come from within. Not until they learn to suppress these discouraging thoughts and replace them with positive and motivating ones will they feel comfortable on the doubles court.

Positive thoughts bring positive results. Very few things can affect the outcome of a match more than what the players involved are thinking. What people think has such a profound effect on them that it actually shapes them into the person that they are. *Attitudes* are the way people act, feel, and think and are determined by what each of us habitually thinks about. The beauty of your attitude is that it can be shaped or molded as you desire by simply controlling what you think about. Doubles players are as positive about themselves and their team as they want to be and will play that way as a result!

ℚ *BELIEVING IN YOURSELVES*

Players who attempt not to lose on the court often find their muscles tight and tense in a shield of defense. Rarely will they reach their playing peak until they discover that trying to play their best instead is what will help them produce more flow and grace in their strokes and style. Belief in themselves will help them to further instill the necessary confidence and charge them toward victory.

Learning to trust in yourselves is the initial step toward playing the game in "automatic." Tennis played in automatic is also referred to as "in the zone." This is the ideal performing state when conscious thoughts on strokes give way to subconscious belief in them. Everything just happens so effortlessly with little thought that players in this state appear to be calmly confident.

Since everyone playing the game of tennis has strengths and weaknesses, it is essential for you to measure your team's abilities by your strengths and *not* your weaknesses. When trying to develop confidence in yourselves, the single biggest obstacle for your team to overcome is how to handle your team's weaknesses. This is where most players concentrate their energies. They are often so insecure with the team's deficiencies and those of the individuals involved that they rarely afford themselves the opportunity to think beyond them.

Practice is the training ground for developing belief in yourselves and your team. It is here, on the practice court, that repetition builds stronger strokes as well as confidence. When minor setbacks befall your team during actual play, learn to think beyond them. Believe in yourselves and the result you know you're capable of, and errors and other minor setbacks will become little challenges your team loves to overcome. You will get back what you program into your computer minds, so believe in yourselves and it is so!

℺ WINNING WITH AWARENESS

Sensible play results from *awareness*. Errors can even be deemed "intelligent" ones when they are quickly analyzed, corrected, and not repeated. Your ability to remain aware, to size up the situation by stepping back and viewing it, will enable you to stay abreast of what is occurring with all four players on the doubles court.

From the warm-up until the last point of the match has been played, your senses will continually gather valuable insight on what is happening. Probe for weaknesses in your opponents. Everyone has them. If you could learn to spot one little weakness and take advantage of it, you'd probably beat most of the players you're currently losing to! The weaknesses may not be obvious, so you might have to tune your awareness to discover them. Maybe your opponents are quite good volleyers at the net. But do they play the ball well at all heights, angles, speeds, and sides? Search . . . it's there for you to find.

Instead of dwelling on your own mistakes, look to those of your opponents. Why are they missing the shots they are?

How are they beating you when they are? What are they doing that's so difficult for you to handle? Learn from your *mistakes* as well as those of your opponents, just as you should learn from the *winners* taking place on the court.

Each of you should strive to help the other by sharing the knowledge gathered throughout the match. Is your team losing control of the ball? Are you losing control of yourselves? Are you straying from the established game plan? Have you discovered an impotency in your opponents' play? Work together to remain in control. Your awareness, if sharply in tune and properly communicated, could be the catalyst to bring out intelligent doubles play within yourselves.

♀ TAKING CONTROL OF YOUR OPPONENTS

The question to ask yourselves is: "Are our opponents really so good or do we just make them look that way?"

Most players experiencing "off" days rarely take into account the shots their opponents are feeding to them. They might miss their backhand long over the baseline and proceed to belittle and berate themselves, instead of crediting their clever opponent for placing the ball to their weaknesses. This is probably the reason most players in tennis feel they should have won after losing. They will convince themselves that it was due to their own poor play (and quite possibly this is true) but neglect to take into account the real cause of their poor play — their crafty opponents. Your opponents will either direct balls to your "likes" or to your "dislikes." When balls are played to your "likes" you will usually credit yourself with the victory. However, when your opponents place shots to your "dislikes" you probably discredit yourself and rarely give credit to your opponent. It is important for you and your partner to realize that players generally play as well as their opponents allow them to and in the future take notice of how well you allow your opponents to play.

Never stray far from the wise old saying, "You should never change a winning game." Strategists love to conjure up new game plans so much that they sometimes forget to follow this sound advice. When your control of the match begins to slip, a change in strategy is necessary. Remember, to turn the tables in the match and have the control swing your way, you will need to make your opponents play differently. To accomplish this, you will probably need to play differently yourselves!

Exploit the weaknesses in your opponents. There are four strokes on the opposite side (each player's forehand and backhand). Find the weakest and place your shots there more often. There are two opponents on the other side of the net. Attack the weakest link in the opposing team. By doing so you will not only break the confidence in the individual player but also in the opposing team. Opponent control is often best executed by exposing the other team's lack of teamwork.

Intimidate them. Hard balls hit close or at them can dampen aggressive play in your opponents and help to keep them under control. This should always be accomplished in a sportsmanlike manner and a "no harm intended" gesture should be made at the completion of the point.

Make them play the way they don't want to play. If they prefer the net, force them to stay on the baseline instead, with deeper strokes and lobs. If they enjoy the game from the baseline, play short balls which pull them into the net. Players who are most comfortable with little movement should be jerked all about the court, while cat-like players who prowl should be tamed with balls directed at them.

You and your partner should always attempt to place the shots to your opponents to give you the shots *you* want. Let's say that you're at the net and your opponents keep lobbing successfully over your heads into the open court for winners. Place balls deeper in the court forcing short replies, so that you can enjoy the easy put-away overheads you prefer. You could also play to the weakest stroke of your opponents or make the slower one stretch out wide for your shot on your next trip to the net. Either way, you'll increase your chances of playing the shot you desire, which in this case is the short lob. If you're wanting a volley instead and your opponents are lobbing you to death, the next time you move in, stay back several steps from your normal aggressive net position to force your opponents away from the lob. Chances are by altering your court position slightly you'll force your opponents to pass, which can give you the very shot you wanted to play, a volley.

ℚ *PLAY YOUR OPPONENTS, NOT YOURSELVES*

When played in control, the game of doubles is a joy for teammates to share. It is a wondrous feeling when two can come together as one on the doubles court. Realistically though, you must recognize that as a team, you will probably experience your share of hard knocks on the road to success. It is times of strife and struggle that will surely test your team's composure. Remain calm and try not to place too much pressure on yourself or your partner when behind in matches. Often the answer to poor play could simply be that, as a team, you're making too many mistakes. Get control of yourselves. Loosen up and relax, slow down your breathing and your walk. Stop pressing your strokes and attempt to smooth them out and let them flow.

Frustrations can often be directed toward your partner during heated play. When difficult moments on the court occur, players have been known to vent their emotions either toward themselves or their partner. Watch out! This is an automatic defeater for your team. When you start playing against yourselves, your team is doomed. Learn to get control of your emotions on court. Don't forget that it is your opponents you are playing, not yourselves. No one likes to lose, especially to themselves!

ℚ *SUMMARY*

Discipline yourself to play the game you desire. Take full responsibility for your actions on the court and look for the answers in your play within yourself. Concentration will never come by force. You must relax yourself and block out past and future thoughts to allow your mind to focus clearly on the task. When problem strokes arise, search for a better understanding by realizing what is taking place at contact. You will probably become the tennis player that your thoughts allow you to be! Don't put yourself and your partner down . . . pick yourselves up with positive thoughts.

Confident players enjoy the luxury of experiencing "automatic tennis." They believe in themselves so they learn to let go and relax, and in the process play the best tennis they're capable of. Tune your awarenesses in sharply to get the most out of what is taking place on the doubles court. With four players competing, the ones who will be winning will likely be the ones most aware of what each and every one is doing. Are your opponents really so good or are you just making them look that way? To make your opponents play differently you will need to play differently yourselves. Generally, all players play as well as their opponents allow them to. Gain control of yourself and your emotions so you don't end up being your own opponent when difficult moments occur. Don't look to blame your partner either; he is on "your side." Don't forget, your real opponents are across the net!

CHAPTER 4

Positioning for Success

⚘ *TAKING ADVANTAGE OF THE NET*

Doubles is a game that is usually won or lost at the net. To have the net means to have the advantage in doubles. In singles play, matches can be won from the baseline at almost every level, however, in doubles, as the level of play increases, getting to the net becomes an increasingly important factor. Like volleyball, players positioned at the net are ready to "spike" the ball down to win the point, while those positioned in the backcourt merely set the point up. The object in doubles is to keep the ball down at the opponent's feet. He is then forced to hit the ball "up" which allows players to close in to the net and hit the rising ball "down" to win the point.

Many players aspiring to master the game of doubles fall short since they are afraid of the net. The ball comes faster to them at the net since their opponents are now positioned closer and they feel their reaction time isn't quick enough to handle the rapid net exchanges. Club players often resolve to stay on the baseline, coming into the net every now and then (rarely ever serving and volleying). If they truly want to start improving their doubles game, they must start coming to the net! If not during match play, then especially in practice in order to feel more secure at the net.

Teach yourself and your partner the volley for the best success of your team. It is actually easier to volley than it is to hit groundstrokes. There is no backswing to be concerned with at the net, just a simple shoulder turn will position your

47

racket properly. There is also little follow-through to worry about. Extend your racket out to make contact well in front of your body and the angle of the racket face will dictate where the ball will travel. Footwork and positioning of your feet aren't as crucial at the net as they are at the baseline either. Using the "1 Step Rule" players are able to reach most balls while positioned at the net. With one cross-over step it is much easier to cover the court from the net than it is from the baseline where many steps are required. And by being closer to the net you'll also have less difficulty hitting over it!

Ideally, doubles is best played when players attempt to take over the net at every opportunity. At the highest level of tennis, all four players are positioned at the net at the close of the point with typically the winning point going to the serving team arriving at the net first. To gain control of the court, start by getting to the net more often. Serve to the weaker side of your opponent (or down the middle if the weaker side cannot be found) and follow your serve to the net. You will never become proficient at serving and volleying until you practice it more often. Staying at the baseline when your volley is weak is not a bad strategy, however, to advance your doubles game you and your partner will eventually need to learn to "like" playing the net.

Taking over the net behind your return of serve can also gain your team the advantage. A "chip and charge" game plan is often the best method to accomplish this. Shorten your stroke by raising your backswing slightly higher and hitting down through the back side of the ball in an abbreviated stroke. With a "chip" shot, balls have backspin and will remain lower after they've bounced on your opponents' side; this forces your opponent to hit up to your waiting volley at the net.

Two players at the net have only nine more feet of court to cover than a singles court. It's very difficult to pass a lone player in singles so when two players are positioned at the net in doubles, it presents an even greater challenge for opponents. Also, by developing an attacking game of doubles, it brings with it an intimidation factor. Additional pressures will be placed on your opponents when you play aggressively. If playing the net is not yet your forte, work to develop your volley. Practice, practice, practice! It's your future to better doubles.

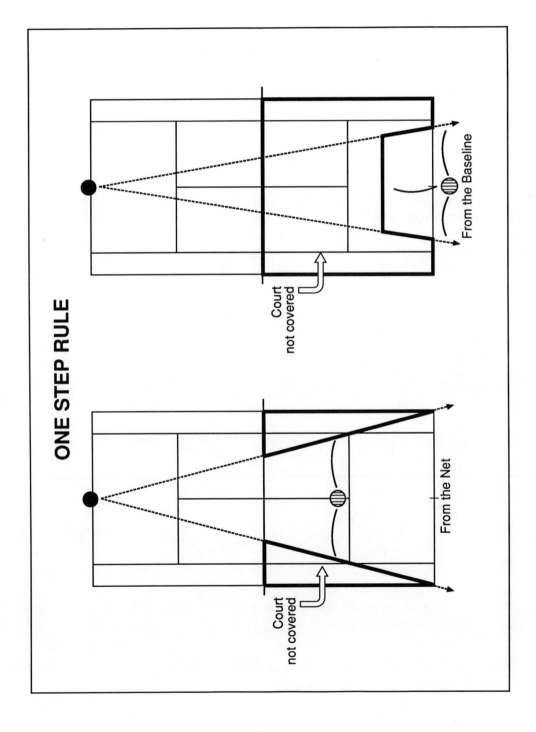

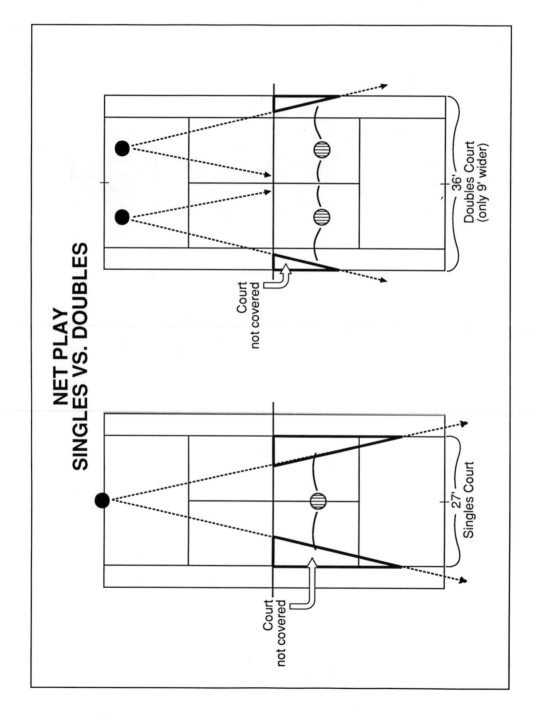

NET PLAY
SINGLES VS. DOUBLES

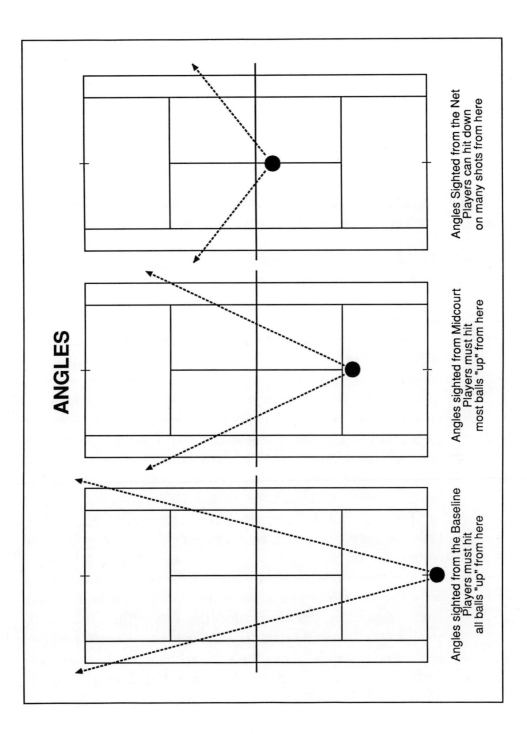

ANGLES

Angles Sighted from the Net
Players can hit down
on many shots from here

Angles sighted from Midcourt
Players must hit
most balls "up" from here

Angles sighted from the Baseline
Players must hit
all balls "up" from here

♋ UNDERSTANDING ANGLES

To better understand why net play is most advantageous in doubles will require an understanding of angles. The next time you are on court, position yourself on the baseline and affix your eyes to the top of the net in front of you. From here, the only part of the court visible on the other side will be that which is seen under or through the net. If the net was completely covered or blocked out, you wouldn't even be able to see the baseline on the opposing side! Keep your eyes on the top of the net and slowly walk in its direction. As you approach the net notice how the court on the other side begins to grow. Continue walking forward and the court seems wider and wider. You can now begin to look down over the net without having to cheat by looking through it to see the court. This is why the top players in the game strive to get to the net. They realize that there is more court for them to hit into because they understand the angles of the court. Doubles really isn't an effective game from the baseline because there is no chance to hit down from there; the angles of the court don't allow it.

When your team understands angles, you will be able to take better control of the points that you play. Wide hit balls often come back wide, while shots played down the center of the court are readily returned down the center. To thwart a good passing team, simply keep more balls in the center of their court to take away the angles that they will be able to play. A serve and volleyer's best success could even come by simply serving all balls down the center of the court to force more returns back down the center. This allows the net person the opportunity to poach a little more easily since more balls will be returned in the center of the court and not out wide of his reach.

Another angle important to consider is where to stand to return serve. A correct stance should be in the middle of the angle created by the server and the service box that he is serving into. Draw an imaginary line between yourself and the server and it should bisect the service box when you're in the correct position. If not properly bisected, you could be inviting an "ace" to appear!

While Stan Smith is positioning to play the ball overhead, his partner, Bob Lutz, quickly moves with him to cover behind.

When Robert Seguso poaches a volley, notice that Ken Flach switches to cover the court left vacant. Rarely will these two ever be found in the "I" formation.

♀ MOVING TOGETHER

Players who learn to "move with the ball" will find themselves in the correct position to cover their opponents' hits more often. By shifting over with wide hit balls, players diminish their opponents' chances of passing them up the alley. However, when one player shifts and the other remains stationary, a gaping hole develops down the middle of the court. With lower level players this hole is often so big that a freight truck could be driven through it! Since the lowest part of the net is located in the center of the court and most shots in doubles are played there, it is vitally important for players to move together to eliminate holes and gaps that can be created when positioned improperly.

The best way to visualize your team's movement is to think that a rope is tied between you. When one of you is pulled out wide for a shot, the other shifts equal distance towards the center in the same direction. Once the shot is played and your partner recovers back to position, you will likewise recover your original position. This rope trick should also be applied to your team's forward and backward movement during play. When one retreats for a lob, both should go back to cover it. And when one advances into the net, both should go in together, as a team.

♀ BALANCING THE COURT

Teams that learn to play *parallel* are stronger than those that prefer the common one up/one back formation. Why? There is a huge diagonal area left open when the players are staggered one up and one back. Opposing teams can quickly take advantage of this powerless formation by directing angled strokes between them.

To balance the tennis court properly requires that the players be aware of designated "zones" and supply coverage to them. Just like defensive backfielders in football and outfielders in baseball, doubles players use zone coverage to position themselves properly to cover all balls in the playing area. When one player gets out of position, it will then be important for the other to help cover the undefended zone.

Whose ball is it when a lob gets over the head of one of the players at the net? Initially it is the responsibility of the

Wendy Turnbull and John Lloyd have been a successful mixed doubles pair over the years. Notice how they are in perfect balance while positioned at the net.

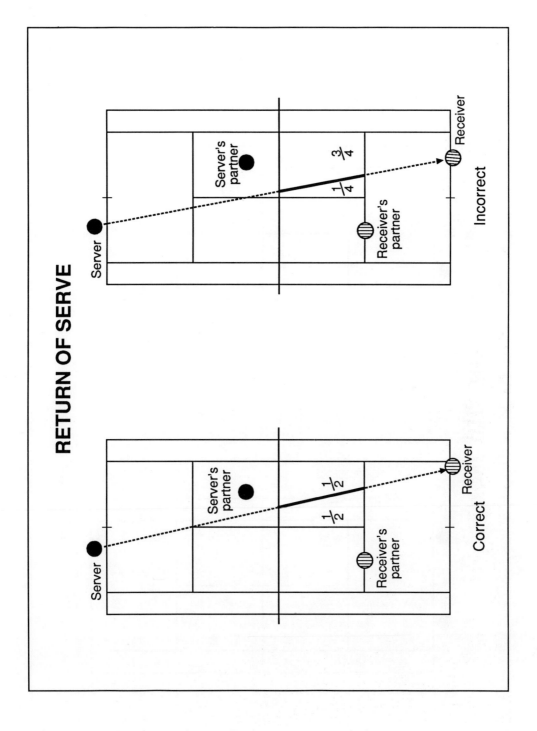

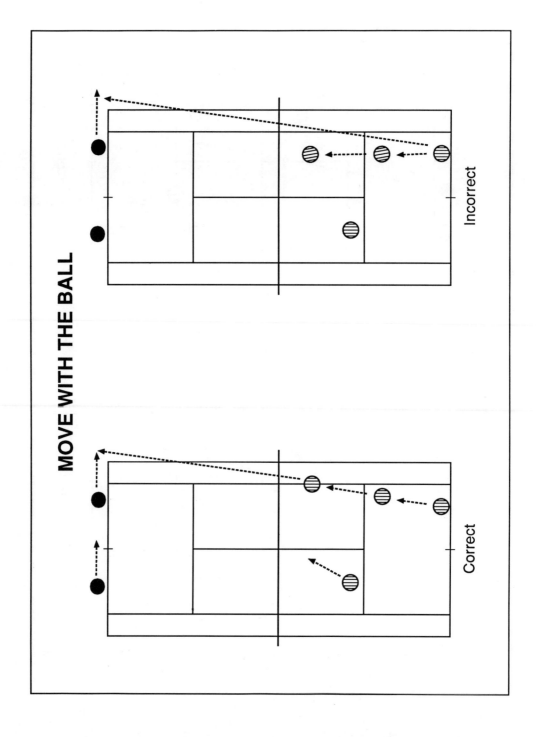

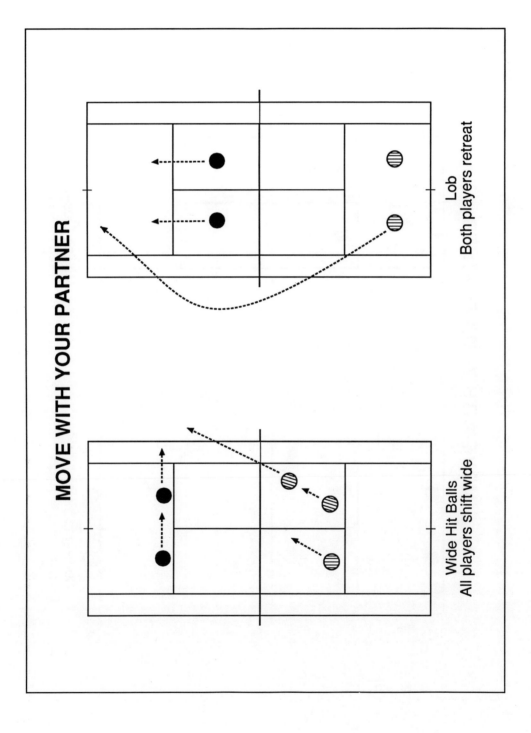

MOVE WITH YOUR PARTNER

Lob
Both players retreat

Wide Hit Balls
All players shift wide

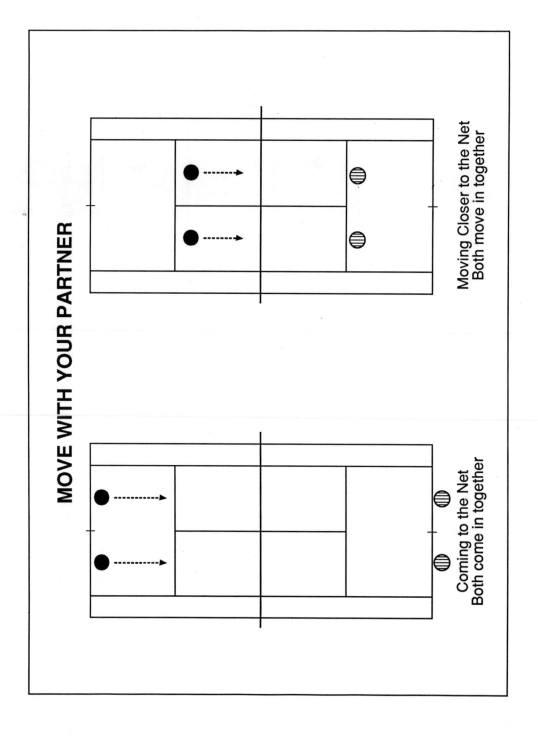

MOVE WITH YOUR PARTNER

Coming to the Net
Both come in together

Moving Closer to the Net
Both move in together

person whose head the ball cleared. However, if he is quick to decide he cannot get to it and properly communicates "Yours" to his partner in time, the ball becomes the responsibility of the assisting partner. This is assuming that the lob cleared the net person's head in a straight line which makes the partner's approach to the ball from the side a better angle and an easier shot to play.

The "I Formation" is the single biggest imbalancing threat to players, and teams should learn to guard against it. The "I Formation" occurs when one player is positioned in front of the other with the other half of the court left vacant. When one players shifts his position to the other side of the court going after a shot, the partner must keep the balance of the team intact by moving over to cover the side left vacant. When "Switch" is quickly communicated, players then recognize which zone they are to cover and move to balance the court.

♀ READING THE BALL

To best position yourselves for the shots you are about to play, learn to "read the ball." It will often let you know if your team should move forward into an offensive position or signal you to retreat in defense even before your opponent strikes the ball. By *anticipating* what the ball will force your opponent to do, you can gain valuable foresight to best position yourselves time and time again.

Balls placed deep in the court to your opponents, hit hard to them or with lots of spin should indicate your control over the point and allow freedom to move in and take command of the net. Balls placed low to opponents' feet, to the weaker opponent, or to weaker strokes will be the sign for your team to alter its position to take advantage of what is likely to occur. On the other hand, short, weaker, or softly played strokes offer control of the point to your opponents. Your best defense could be to retreat backward or to brace yourself for an anticipated offensive shot coming your way.

Keep your eye on the ball to all players on the court at all times. Watch the effects it has on each and how everyone reacts to its many varying speeds, bounces, and placements. Your awareness of how the ball controls those on the court will certainly advance you toward becoming the intelligent doubles player that you want to be.

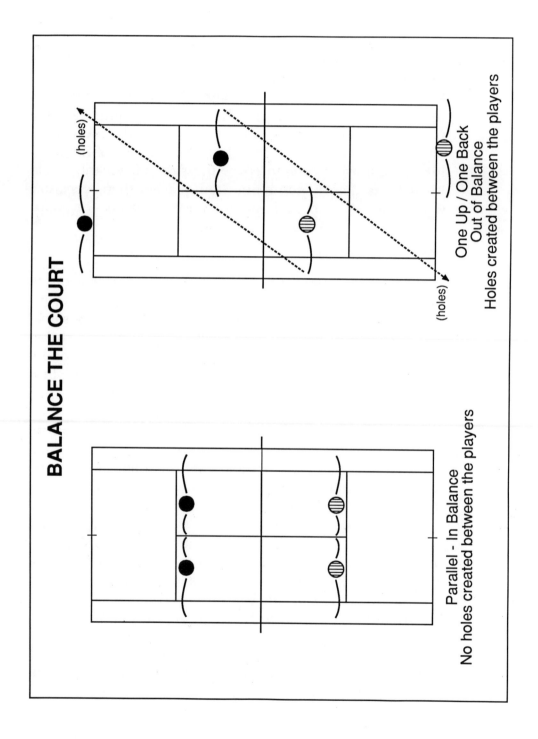

BALANCE THE COURT

One Up / One Back
Out of Balance
Holes created between the players

(holes)

(holes)

Parallel - In Balance
No holes created between the players

Even as your partner strikes the ball, keep your eyes on it all the way to his racket (quickly glance over your shoulder if he is positioned behind you). You will better react to the shot he is about to play once you learn to anticipate what the ball will make your partner do. Once you see that the ball has allowed him to make a more effective shot, move in before your opponents have a chance to reply. You'll be able to take advantage of the position created when successful at reading the ball. You'll also discover that you'll automatically become much quicker as balls will seem easier to reach when you are ideally positioned each time.

ADJUSTING YOUR POSITIONS

One of the most common mistakes in doubles is for players to assume the same position on the court each time they play. They routinely stand to serve from the same spot, receive from their favorite place each time, and as their partner serves or receives the ball, anchor themselves in their established location time and time again. What these players need to understand is that not all players are alike, and the various positions they are assuming on the doubles court should vary with the different players they compete against.

Beginners of the game of doubles learn where to stand on the court to be properly positioned for each role they are to play. As a server, players are generally taught to stand behind the baseline out wider than they would in a singles match, since they now have a partner to help cover the other half of the court. The server's partner is stationed approximately in the center of the service box at the net. The receiver is on the opposite side on the baseline (or a step behind it) while the receiver's partner stands on the middle of the service line at the adjacent service box. From here they are taught to play the game and quite often, from here they continue to play the game . . . for a lifetime!

There is really no one *right* position in doubles. The best positions in doubles will come through using your heads! Don't settle in the same place to serve each time, alter your positions to get the best angles and results possible. As a receiver, your position will most likely be dictated by the server's position and ability. Analyze her stroke to discover the ideal spot from which to receive. As the partner of the server

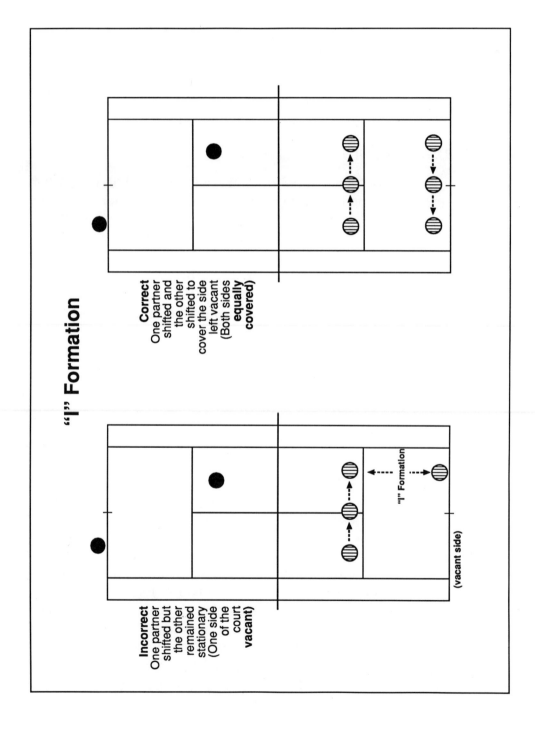

"I" Formation

Incorrect
One partner shifted but the other remained stationary (One side of the court **vacant**)

(vacant side)

"I" Formation

Correct
One partner shifted and the other shifted to cover the side left vacant (Both sides **equally covered**)

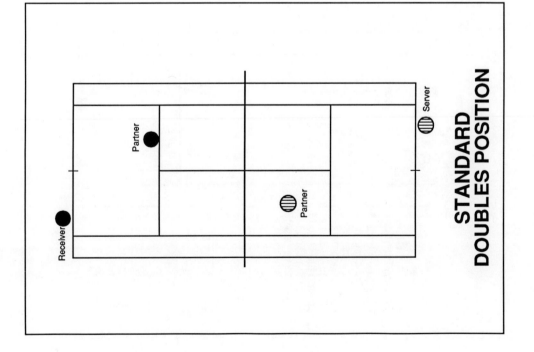

STANDARD DOUBLES POSITION

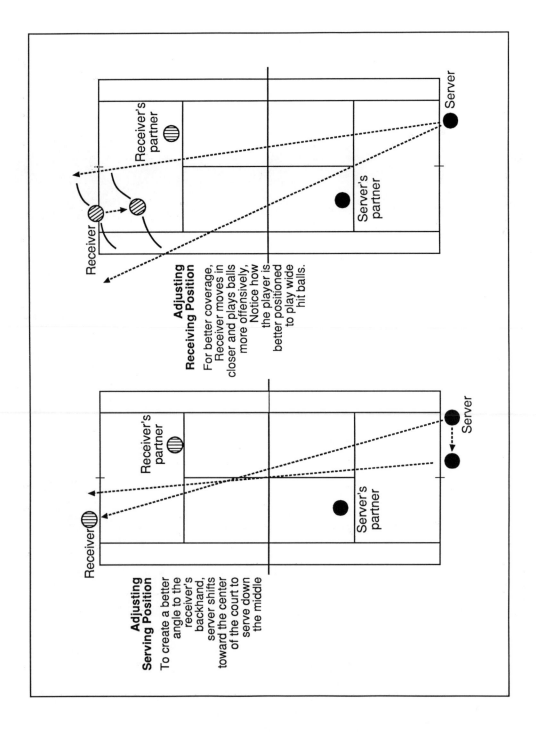

Adjusting Receiving Position

For better coverage, Receiver moves in closer and plays balls more offensively. Notice how the player is better positioned to play wide hit balls.

Adjusting Serving Position

To create a better angle to the receiver's backhand, server shifts toward the center of the court to serve down the middle and receiver, move in when the time necessitates aggression and move back when playing defense. Learn to refrain, however, from simply "camping out" in the same place each time.

Servers having a difficult time playing effective serves down the middle to receivers' backhands or weaker strokes should position themselves much closer to the center service mark when serving. They need not worry so much about covering their side of the court since an inside-out or reverse crosscourt backhand (or weak side) stroke is an extremely difficult shot for their opponents to master.

Receivers should also look to alter their positions by moving in as close inside the baseline as they can. Normally players are seen receiving from the ineffective location several steps behind the baseline. From here, not only is it more difficult for receivers to make offensive returns, but it also gives the server the advantage of being able to pull the receiver out of position on wide hits. Balls that "kick" with good topspin also force difficult replies from receivers positioned back too far as they struggle, attempting to play the ball at shoulder height. When the receiver moves in several steps *inside* the baseline, he can take the serve early and send it back sooner leaving the serving team less time to prepare for it. This is especially true for *second* serves. When the server misses the first serve, the receiving team must make them pay for it! The receiving team should then move in together and pressure the serving team by beating them to the net. This strategy will often increase the number of double faults as the server attempts to end the "net takeover attempt" by serving deeper or more powerfully than he feels comfortable with.

Net partners normally adjust their positions upon seeing what shots have been played. They step toward the alley on wider hit shots and toward the center on balls played down the middle of the court. They look to move in more when non-lobbing patterns of play exist and back up slightly to shield against the lob when it is being used frequently. They alter their level of intensity when in the ready position to match the speed of the game being played. They will even completely change the location of their stance by joining their partner on the baseline should their strategy necessitate such a plan of defense.

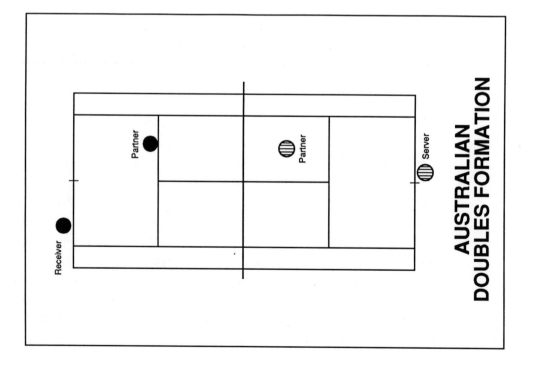

**AUSTRALIAN
DOUBLES FORMATION**

✑ CREATIVE DOUBLES

Often, a change in formation is exactly what the doctor (local pro) ordered and can be used to turn a match completely around. Once patterns of play have been established and trends discovered, look to alter them and take control of the play by making changes to the positions of your team. It just might prove to be the strategy needed to get your team back on the winning track.

Australian doubles is a great tool to use to "throw off" your opponents. The server will stand close to the center service mark behind the baseline while his partner shifts to stand in the other service box. With this new formation, the receiver's favorite crosscourt shot is taken away and he is forced to make the more difficult down-the-line return. This is an effective way to keep your opponents off balance by mixing up the play and forcing them to make uncomfortable returns. Once they settle in and feel "grooved" playing against your team in this new position, switch back to your regular position. Continue your control of the match by switching back and forth from your regular to Australian positions until your opponents are completely uncomfortable with their play.

When all else fails and your team finds itself faltering badly, look to switch sides with your partner at the close of the set. This new change might be the answer to your team's woes. You could even change which partner serves first in the new set. By learning to experiment a little more, you might discover more success thorough your team's own creativity!

✑ SUMMARY

Get yourself and your partner up to the net. Reach your best by using the net position to your advantage. Understand how to get and use angles for successful doubles play. Move into the proper position with your partner by visualizing a rope tied between you. Don't let holes and gaps occur by moving independently of each other. Balance the court by playing parallel to one another. Avoid the "I Formation" like the plague!

Some of your most intelligent play will come from effectively "reading the ball." Learn how it affects everyone on the court to successfully anticipate the correct position. Vary the position you and your partner assume by adjusting it according to the various players you're competing against. The ideal position for your team will be found by using your heads to discover it. Be prepared to change your position completely should it be necessary to gain control of the match. "Pull out all the stops" by learning to bring out your team's creativity. Your success might just depend on it!

CHAPTER 5

Achieving Consistent Results

⚲ *THE PERCENTAGES ARE IN BASIC DOUBLES*

The team that plays the *percentages* in doubles will have the most favorable odds to perform well consistently. Players who understand and apply the basic principles of sound doubles play will repeatedly be in the winners' circle. Understand the basics of doubles and apply them to your own games:

1. *The Better Server Serves First.*
   Your team needs to get off to a good start and if the set is close, this allows the better server to help your team win it at the end.

2. *Get a High Percentage of First Serves in.*
   Statistics prove that many more points are won when *first* serves are hit in. It also helps to keep the pressure on your opponents.

3. *Serve Down the Middle of the Court.*
   Limit the receivers' angle by forcing them to keep the return in the center of the court. This will also provide the opportunity for your partner to poach.

4. *Hold Serve!*
   If your team doesn't lose its serve, you can't lose the match! It's that simple.

5. *Strive for Consistent Returns.*
   Get all returns back into play. Don't give points away to

your opponents with your return errors. Treat returns with the same care as you normally do with second serves.

6. *Keep the Ball in the Middle of the Court.*
   The net is lower there and it takes away the angle of your opponents.

7. *Lob if in Doubt.*
   It can be your best defense against aggressive play. It can also help your team eliminate errors.

8. *Take Over the Net.*
   Use the position at the net to your team's advantage by hitting down from there to win the points.

9. *The Team with the Fewest Errors Wins!*
   It's not winners that win matches, it's error-free play.

10. *Change a Losing Game and Never One that's Winning.*
    Learn to change your game to do what it takes to win.

⚲ *USING RELIABLE STROKES*

Balls that are crushed with huge windup swings and aimed close to the lines have little chance of producing consistent results in tennis. It is slow, steady, and confident swings that bring success on the court. Consistency blended with aggressive play is the winning combination needed in doubles.

The two strokes that begin points in tennis for every team are the *serve* and the *return of serve.* It is especially important to develop reliable strokes with these two. The most consistent and accurate strokes with which your team starts the point will usually score the most consistent results in the end. Allow the other team to gamble by going for the lines and trying to end points quickly with unnecessary winners; avoid this style of play yourselves.

Cannonball serves should be spared for the singles court in your attempt to record a higher percentage of *first* serves in play. When first serves repeatedly land in the service box, opponents are left frustrated. However, when the first serve falters, opponents relax and become confident with their return of the second serve. Not only is the pressure off of your opponents when your first serve misses, but it also wears and tires your body as the match progresses since you must attempt to serve so many more balls. Players who have "cream puff" second serves should strive to develop more reliable medium-paced ones which are more effective and less vulnerable.

Don't be afraid to attempt shots in tennis, however, do play within yourself. Play the game that you're confident in and capable of. Avoid unnecessary gambles and unreasonable risks with your play. Remember that power comes *after* placement and control in doubles. Use your most reliable strokes and your team will have the consistent results you desire.

℘ *PLACING THE BALL FOR SUCCESS*

Every shot in tennis should be hit with a purpose in mind. A target must be conceived in the player's mind before a hit is made to achieve success with the placement of the ball. Balls aren't directed aimlessly about the court in hopes of good fortune. They are predetermined or predirected, if you will, by the players involved. Luck is then *made* through the use of intelligence on the tennis court; rarely will it happen by chance.

Smart players realize which shots their opponents don't like. They analyze their every move by constantly probing for weaknesses. Once they've discovered them, you can bet the ball will be skillfully directed to these weaknesses. Obviously, such clever players understand and have control of the ball but they've taken their games another level. They have learned to uncover and exploit weaknesses in their opponents.

Your mind, the computer that it is, can be programmed to think out several moves in advance much like a chess player. With advance planning of where your shots will go, your mind will avoid common worries like "Where should the ball be directed now?" during match play. Once your opponents' weaknesses have been discovered and you and your partner have planned your strategy accordingly, it will be easier to direct the ball there automatically and with intention. If new weaknesses are later discovered, set your plan once again in motion with your partner and reprogram your minds for a new plan of attack. New targets must be programmed into your thoughts so you and your partner will be prepared to place the ball strategically and automatically at those targets during play.

♕ THERE ARE NO EASY SHOTS

The difference in the levels of tennis players is often measured not by their strokes but rather by their ability (or inability) to handle the "easy shots" effectively. UNFORCED ERRORS KILL! They are out to ruin every tennis player's game and are quite cancerous once they attack. Your best defense against this is to sharpen your concentration as well as your awareness of what is taking place on the tennis court. Don't let routine errors destroy your game. They'll help you beat yourself if you let them.

Players in the game of doubles often perform with the intensity and zest of spirited fighters. They charge about the court and challenge themselves to the many difficult tasks they confront. They will often rise to the occasion when called upon, but at the same time can relax their guard when the challenge becomes less exciting. Everyone who has ever played the game has experienced some form of concentration lapse. Players tend to lose their fighting edge when their intensity begins to lag and their desire usually diminishes along with it. These players might appear quite sharp when match play warrants it but let dull, less demanding play ensue and watch these same players plummet.

Players in general tend to play the game too tensely and often miss shots as they rush through them in the stroking process. These overly intense players often discover that they will repeatedly miss the easy ones as they attempt to overplay them; that is, attempt to do more with the ball than is necessarily required. Easy sitters, for example, hovering over the net, simply call for tapping the ball into the open court to win the point. Forceful players instead attempt to murder the ball with big powerful swings. They would have much more success in the game by learning to match the effort to the task. Don't overplay the ball–that only brings inconsistent results (especially with the easy shots).

Concentration and intensity should be kept at the highest controllable level during all shots. The easy or routine shots should have special attention paid to them since it is here that unforced errors develop. Avoid casual play in yourself and your team. If you must err, make sure that your opponents' forcing play is the cause. Everyone makes mistakes on the court, but you can limit yours by attempting all shots with the same level of intense concentration. You will discover a healthier game once you've rid yourself of so many unforced errors.

℘ PUT AWAY THE PUT-AWAYS!

One of the biggest sins a doubles player commits is when he is in an enviable position at the net able to win the point and then fails to capitalize on it. Not only are mistakes often made on these "sitters" (as we've already seen), but balls are also incorrectly hit directly back to opponents. This offers them another shot at winning the point and it also diminishes your chances of having another such golden opportunity to win it yourself!

"Putting the ball away" isn't the same as hitting a "kill shot." It means placing the ball smoothly and safely to win the point consistently. When correctly positioned at the net, high balls should be directed one of three places: 1) at the net person; 2) between the two opponents; or 3) angled off wide. A common mistake among net players is to send a winning volley back to the waiting baseline player. Since this person is farthest from the ball, logically he has the most time to react to it. The person positioned closer to the net has far less reaction time and therefore is the ideal person to direct the ball to. When the ball is placed at his feet, it isn't likely that he will be able to make any kind of play on it, much less a good one.

By positioning yourselves closer to the net you will see it is much easier to put the ball away. High balls affording you the opportunity to hit down will be more common, and balls aren't as likely to get to your feet from here either. The front 1/3 to 1/2 of the service box is the ideal location to stand. From here you will still be able to cover the lob effectively as well as move forward aggressively to volley out in front.

Learning to put away the put-aways is important to advancing your team's level of play. Use the entire width of the court to create the best angle that wins the point. Use safety and margin of error to accurately place the ball with control. Hit the ball *not to your opponents but away from them.* Do so with intelligence, not power, for consistent winning placements.

♀ AVOIDING HOT/COLD PLAY

Have you ever experienced a day when everything you attempted on the court worked beautifully and the very next day nothing did? This can aptly be described as hot/cold tennis — inconsistent performances. Everyone has good and bad days with their play, however, to become the best team you're capable of will require both of you to understand how to limit your "bad day" performances.

It is inescapably human to err. However, it's only after errors are repeated again and again that they become mistakes in tennis. Players who learn from their errors won't continue to repeat them. They won't experience as many "off days" either, because their minds are aware of what is occurring during play and they are able to make necessary corrective adjustments to their games.

Doubles is not a game of power but of intelligent use of speed. When players try to hit "home runs" on every hit they will discover "hit or miss" syndrome. Although the great Babe Ruth was a legendary home run hitter in baseball, he also held the strikeout record! What does this say about his consistency?!

When a doubles pair learns to be *complementary* they have the best shield against hot/cold play. When one is hitting errors and making mistakes, the other needs to play higher percentage shots to compensate for the partner's poor play. Alley shots, difficult drop angles, or strokes hit with brute strength should be avoided at this time. It is the partner's duty to get the team back on the winning track by getting a few more balls into play and in the process help his partner get his rhythm back. This play might be required for only a few points or possibly an entire match. Players must be ready to adapt their game according to what the situation calls for and the needs of the team.

When the players of a tandem are of mixed levels, each will have a job to do to help the team perform well consistently. The stronger player or captain of the team should take charge by roving the net more, forcing the opponents, and ending the points with put-away shots. The weaker player also has an important task to perform. He lobs more, is as consistent with keeping the balls in play as possible, and follows the tactical plan set by the captain. He attempts to get all balls back over the net and into the court (not into the net!) to give the team the best chance of winning the points they play.

A pair is weakest when the players neglect to work together. If a server is left to fend for himself without the help of the net person his chances of success are minimal. When a player experiences a period of poor play and his partner isn't able to recognize or take up the slack for the team at this needed time, how will they ever hope to win? They must learn to complement each other, help one another, and work together to avoid inconsistent play in themselves. If your partner's game begins to falter, don't blame him. Recognize that the team needs your help at this time and alter your game to get the team back in control. There will surely be other times when your game will flounder and your partner will be the one needed to help the team to victory. Don't look to *blame* your partner when he is in trouble, look to *help* him and your team play well consistently.

♀ ADAPTABLE STRATEGIES

When you and your partner insist on playing the same game against all opponents, chances are that unless your team is invincible it will record its share of losses. Your team needs to be *adaptable* in its play to win regularly. Against some opponents the game that you and your partner normally play just might be the best one to use in order to defeat them. However, against others, it might not prove to be the correct one. Your team, therefore, must be prepared to play differently in order to win. Different opponents have different weaknesses so you and your partner will need to alter your games to exploit them in each of the opponents you face.

The best way to keep your opponents off balance is to play a game that is *unpredictable*. Keep them guessing with a wide variety of shots. If the opposing net player is picking off your routine crosscourt shots, alter your hits by lobbing, hitting down the alley, or with sharper angles crosscourt. Don't let them get comfortable with your play.

To change your team's strategy might require you to alter

the position you and your partner are playing, change the direction of the targets of your shots, or change your style of play (i.e., offensive to defensive). Whatever the case, you and your partner must be willing to vary your games to meet the demands of the various opponents you will encounter. Your team's ability to recognize what strategy is necessary to win, as well as its openness to changing the game accordingly, will play a big role in the future successes of your team.

♀ *CONSISTENT HABITS PRODUCE CONSISTENT GAMES*

What you and your partner do on a regular basis will ultimately establish the game you will each play. The way you prepare for matches, what you think about during play, the strokes you hit most often, as well as your level of concentration, all make you into the unique players you are. Your attitude is also determined by the habits you have established for yourselves. Once you learn to make them more consistent, you will discover that your play will become that way as well.

Make positive thinking on the court a habit. Strive to achieve your highest level of concentration by relaxing and letting go more often. Believe in yourselves on a regular basis. Prepare properly both physically and mentally for consistent results. Play the controlled game of tennis that is within you each time.

Another important habit to develop in your play is to become more *patient.* Patient players understand what *opportunistic waiting* is all about. This is often what keeps junior players performing like "kids." They lack patience in their strokes and style of play and as a result make many senseless errors. Tennis is a game of cat-and-mouse and the players involved must be able to wait for the right moment for the "kill." Too early and it could leave players vulnerable to making unnecessary errors. Since doubles is a game won or lost on mistakes, waiting for the right moment (to avoid making errors) is an important concern for your team's success.

Your play will be as consistent as the habits you set for yourselves. If your team has been experiencing its share of losses or poor play, look to the habits of each player and the team as a whole. Are you happy with what you see? If not, try to develop winning habits in yourselves. It will take an effort on your part, but it will be attainable through your team's discipline and determination.

⚘ BECOME A BORING CHAMPION

I've given countless lessons to "flashy" players on how to be a little more *boring* on the doubles court. Although it's an abrupt change in style, these players all seem to become much better doubles players once they've shed their "pizzazz" to find consistent play in themselves.

Aces, winners, and other big shots offer great short-term rewards but seldom consistent results in doubles. It's not screaming shots off the line that make players into champions, it's well-placed balls day in and day out.

The next time you're out playing doubles, slow down your game! Relax . . . don't rush about the court. Plan your strokes by allowing a comfortable margin for error on each and then execute them smoothly and safely. Let your strokes and your stride flow. Eliminate your unforced errors by getting the maximum ball control from each shot you attempt. Play strokes that offer the greatest percentage chance of success. Stay away from temptations of power, hitting lines, and other heroic play!

Leave the flamboyant play to the singles stars. Slow down and play a controlled game of doubles. You and your partners' ability to make boring shots regularly and to reduce your errors in the process will be what makes you into champions. Even though your play will not make you look like tough opponents, you'll be winning matches consistently on your *wits* and not your appearance.

⚘ SUMMARY

Understanding and playing *basic doubles* can bring your team consistent results. Use strokes you can rely on. Don't attempt unrealistic shots you don't feel comfortable making. Place the ball to the targets you and your partner have deemed best in your strategic planning. This will help keep you focused on where the next ball should be directed. Play the easy shots just as you would the difficult ones. Don't let your concentration lapse and your play get sloppy by making senseless errors with the routine shots.

Once you are in position to win the point, do so by placing the ball away from the opponents. Direct the ball to the closest opponent's feet if you are confronted with a higher ball with few available angles. Learn from your errors so you won't continue to repeat them. Avoid inconsistent play by complementing your partner. Help your team play well consistently by helping your partner when he is in need. Adapt your games to develop the winning strategy necessary for each team you play against. Every team is unique and therefore needs a unique game plan to defeat. Be consistent with your habits to play well consistently. Become a boring doubles team that consistently wins without all the flash and pizzazz that temporary stars possess.

CHAPTER 6

The
Midcourt Advantage

♀ *KEEPING THE CONTROL*

Three shots are usually played each time you and your partner approach the net from the baseline position. The first is either a serve or return that you're following into the net behind or an approach shot played from a groundstroke exchange. The second hit usually made in your quest for the net is called a "first volley" or set-up shot. The third stroke is the "second volley" or put-away shot that, we hope, ends the point. If you are extremely quick in your advance to the net, the total number of strokes necessary could even be cut to two. The set-up shot could be eliminated if you're already in a position closer to the net and able to end the point on your first volley attempt. However, this is where most volley mistakes are made. Players try to end the points too *quickly*, especially when they aren't in the proper position to do so with consistent results.

The midcourt is the area located just in front of the service line to just behind it. Since players are closer to the net from this location but still aren't within "striking distance," this position offers them a false sense of command of the net. The result is that more errors occur at the midcourt than any other area on the court. Since the net is easy to see through, it appears as though one can hit down from this location and end the point more quickly. If the net had a dark cloth covering it, the picture would be much clearer to see; the ball must still be hit "up" from here to reach the other side

John Newcombe is shown in the mid-court handling this most difficult shot with care.

successfully. People in general, though, have always preferred to take the easy route or shortcut to accomplish most tasks. This is the primary cause of most errors at the net. When attempts are made to end the point too soon, inconsistent net play will result.

The midcourt position can be used to your advantage by understanding what you need to do at this crucial location. Keep the advantage or *control*, don't try to win the point outright! Stay away from attempting winning shots on your first volley unless you're in the correct put-away position close to the net. Open the face of your racket to lift the ball higher and gain good depth on the placement of your shots. Make percentage shots from here, down the center of the court or to the weaknesses of your opponents (unless an opening is seen elsewhere).

Strategically, this is where the point is set up. Like an assist in basketball, it is the play that sets the basket or winning points up for the next play of the ball. The midcourt area is where control of the point is usually won or lost. Learn to place the ball from here, don't power it! Move closer to the net to end the point on your next stroke. Don't be too anxious to end the point sooner than you should. You'll discover that by being *patient* with this transition shot you'll eliminate many of the errors you may now be making at the net.

☌ BENEFITING FROM THE "CHECK STEP"

Players who find themselves repeatedly passed while at the net need to learn the valuable secret of the *check step*. The check step is a brief stop you will need to make on your way to the net. It is necessary to help you properly position and cover all shots your opponents are hitting. Both feet come down together in the check step with legs spread out approximately as wide as the shoulders. From this ready position you will be prepared to move in the direction of the ball your opponent has hit.

It is important to understand that it is not necessarily a place or line on the court where you need to stop briefly on your movement to the net. Instead, *it is when your opponent makes contact with the ball on her stroke.* Your check step stop should occur each time your opponent strikes the ball no matter what your position on the court. Timing is of utmost

John McEnroe, one of the greatest volleyers in tennis history, is shown "going to the ball". Notice the arm extension and body weight into the shot. His partner, Peter Fleming, quickly moves in to join John at the net during his exchange.

importance. Your eyes should follow the ball to the impact of your opponent's hit to properly prepare for your shortened stop to occur at that exact moment. A check step that is improperly timed will result in poor positioning and inadequate coverage on many balls you attempt to play. When no check step is made, your forward momentum generally pulls you toward the *net* each time and not necessarily in the direction of the *ball!*

In football, the check step is called "breakdown." Players quickly move into this ready position by crouching lower to the ground with slightly bent knees, on their toes, ready to spring into action. Although they aren't reacting to the hit of a ball like in tennis, they are timing their maneuver on changes in the direction the ball is traveling.

The next time you approach the net use more caution. Instead of racing toward the net with abandon and blazing speed, slow down in the midcourt area. You've moved in quickly from the baseline, which is fine, but at the midcourt you now need to slow down and gain body and ball *control.* Use the check step to your advantage. Momentarily freeze at the instant your opponent hits her shot and prepare your body to continue moving, not necessarily in the direction of the net, but in the direction of the *ball!*

⚲ GOING TO THE BALL

The goal of many net rushers is simply to reach the net. What is often forgotten is that they must always go to the *ball* and that might not necessarily be in the direction of the net. That is the reason the check step is so beneficial in doubles. Once players learn to slow down and stop, they are then more focused on the ball and their movement toward it. Covering the entire court is essential. You should never race toward the net in a straight line, playing only those balls hit directly to you. You must move toward the net, stop, and then proceed to move and cover *all balls* played to your side of the court.

You shouldn't guess where the ball will be traveling either. You can learn to anticipate when you *watch* and *read* your opponent and the ball. Don't commit your movement until you've seen the ball come off your opponent's racket. His racket and body movements can also tip you off as to where intended shots are going.

Players volleying in the midcourt often "jab" at the ball on the right or left side as if they were making a stab in the dark. To volley successfully requires a two-part maneuver. The first part pivots the shoulder to position the racket and the second is when the racket and body move forward to meet the ball out in front. Problems occur when players *wait* and volley the ball at their side. The best volleyers have all learned to *go to the ball* to play it early out in front of the body. They move diagonally while at the net for better contacts early out in front and avoid moving parallel to the net in fear of late hits. They understand that more success at the net comes with volleys played in front and they strive *never to allow balls to get to their sides.*

Once you've established a midcourt position, don't back away from the net unless it's a lob. Players who repeatedly retreat find themselves off balance with little weight behind their shots. They should keep the momentum of their body into the hit, not away from it. Learn to go to the ball when volleying; don't wait for it to come to you. Your volleys are sure to improve when you do.

♀ *NOT ON THE RUN*

In your quest for the net, think of your movement as if at a stoplight. Proceed on "green" in between hits, slow to "yellow" and use caution upon your opponent's hit, and prepare to stop at the volley on your own as if it were "red." Your body will be better balanced and in control now that it isn't moving, which allows for better controlled hits.

Net play often requires "stop and go" movements. Players who haven't learned the stoplight theory at the net are sure to experience stroking difficulties while positioned there. Following the check step, continue to the ball; however, once you reach it, *stop.* It is at this time that body control is of utmost importance to produce successful strokes. Moving through the hit only complicates and hinders timing of the ball, which is crucial on the volley.

Move, check step, move, stop to volley. Move, check step, move, stop to volley. Move, check step, move, stop to volley. This is the footwork action to use at the net. Notice how movement only takes place between hits. While each person is stroking the ball is the time to remain momentarily still. It's not as essential to remain motionless when your partner or opponents are stroking the ball, but it's good practice. On your hit, however, ball control is essential, so remain stationary a little longer or until the ball leaves your racket. Learning to control your body and to stop while volleying is sure to help make your volleys a little easier to master.

⚲ DON'T STAND THERE ADMIRING!

After each of your hits, it will be necessary to recover or proceed to the desired position on the court. The worst possible sin you could make at this time is to hit and "stand there admiring" your shot! Poor positioning will result and this offers your opponents opportunities and openings to pass or take command of the point.

The temptation to admire your shots during match play will always be present. Sometimes the hit just feels so good that you want to gain a little pleasure by watching it awhile. Resist the temptation! Hit and *move* into position. You can watch your shot (you should always keep watching the ball) while you're moving but avoid hitting and standing there.

Unless you've hit an outright "winner," you will need to take advantage of making a good shot by moving into the proper position following the hit. The advantage will shift to your opponents if you merely stand there admiring it!

Avoid waiting or pausing after hits you've decided to move into the net behind. On serves and approach shots for example, move continuously throughout the stroke toward the net. This can still be accomplished with sound body control and balance at contact. This practice shouldn't be applied to all strokes, just those that require a greater distance to move in behind them. Extra caution and care should be taken while playing the ball on the move. This is where many errors occur, especially by players attempting this maneuver when it's not necessarily required.

⚲ INCREASE YOUR LEVELS OF INTENSITY

Is your level of intensity or state of readiness the same when attempting to hit a ball traveling 100 miles per hour as it is when you are attempting to hit a ball traveling ten miles per hour? It shouldn't be. Your intensity normally is dictated by the speed of the ball you are playing as well as the proximity of the opponents. Generally, the closer you are to the net, the more intense you should then become.

There are three body cues to take notice of when determining your level of intensity: *elbows, heels,* and *knees.*

While stationed in the ready position, note where your elbows are. Are they inward, toward your body, even along your sides, or are they extended more out in front? Players who are at a lower level of intensity tend to pull their elbows into their body in a more comfortable position. This is fine when at ease or when less intense demands are being placed on the players, however, while at the net, when intensity is usually at its highest, elbows should be extended further out in front of the body. The racket will then be better prepared and in a more desirable position to react more quickly and catch the ball earlier out in front of the body.

Heels touching the ground definitely signal a lower level of intensity. When playing the net, avoid touching your heels to the ground except when striking the ball. Players who stand flat footed while at the net tend to have rigid balance. They could find themselves automatically more intense and ready by coming off their heels and standing more on the balls of their feet. Body weight will shift forward in the process affording better anticipation and readiness. They will now find themselves better prepared for quick net exchanges.

Standing completely upright with locked knees also affects quickness and mobility. Flex your knees slightly to be ready to spring into action. If a slight flex is good, is more knee bending such as a "squat" even better? No! Just a slight knee bend will best prepare your body for quick movements at the net. Deeper knee bends require too much time to fully extend and propel your body about the court.

As you and your partner advance to the midcourt, adjust your intensity levels to compensate for the shorter distance created between you and your opponents. Decide before each exchange where the ball should be directed to avoid unnecessary surprises while rallying. Get your racket heads under control. Firm your grips and wrists to prepare for faster balls coming your way. Extend your elbows and rackets out further in front, get off your heels, and flex your knees slightly in a more intense ready position. Now you're prepared to volley your best and gain the midcourt advantage!

♉ *WHERE MOST DOUBLES MATCHES ARE WON AND LOST*

One of the worst locations you and your partner could ever play the game from is "no person's land." This is the area located between the midcourt area and the baseline. From here, very few shots come easy. Balls seem to be easily directed at players' feet and behind them when they're caught standing in no person's land. This is the very essence of the lesson that "tennis is a game played behind the baseline *or* at the net." Players stroking balls inside the baseline should proceed either *toward the net* after the shot or *retreat behind the baseline* to continue the point.

The midcourt area differs very little from no person's land. This is the reason that the midcourt area is not an ideal position for you and your partner to play the game from. Then why is there an entire chapter devoted to the midcourt area, you ask? Most doubles matches are won and lost from play occurring midcourt. Only very advanced and experienced doubles players understand the importance of shots played from here. Lesser players feel they are close enough for offensive shots and make the majority of their errors here. If they would only be more patient, cautious, and intelligent in their placements, they would discover that the midcourt is a great place to gain not only the advantage but also control of the points they play.

Sure, balls will sometimes be directed at your feet while you're positioned midcourt, however, through the use of more caution and care these difficult shots can be safely directed with consistency. Place low volleys and half volleys well above the net with enough margin for error, away from the lines, and deep enough to control the point. Stay away from aggressively attempting outright winners off balls played at your feet.

The service line is a tempting place to hit glorified winners. Sometimes this might be possible but rarely with consistent success. Even though you might feel close enough for the "kill," resist the temptation because you actually aren't. Try instead to *control the point* and to *keep the pressure on your opponents.* Make them beat you by hitting between you, passing you down the line, or hitting a perfect placement over your heads. Direct your shots so that this will be a difficult task for them to accomplish with any regularity. That is winning with percentage doubles play. The midcourt will prove to be a valuable location for the success of your team once you learn to set your shots up from here. But remember, to gain the benefits of your well placed balls, you and your partner will need to move into a position closer to the net to consistently end the points.

ℚ *SUMMARY*

Keep the advantage or control from the midcourt; don't always try to end the points outright from here. Don't be over anxious to end the points sooner than you should. Use the check step to control your body properly and position yourself to play all balls. Remember, you're going to the *ball* not just the net. Don't wait for the ball to come to you when volleying; go to *it* to contact balls in front and avoid playing them at your side. Although you're always moving to the ball, once you reach it *stop to volley*. Running through the volley certainly makes it a more difficult shot to master no matter what your level of play. Once the volley has been played, move into position.

Avoid the temptation to stand there admiring your well-placed ball. Increase your level of intensity while playing the net. Properly prepare yourself for the quick net exchanges. Play it smart midcourt. You and your partner can choose to use this position to take command of points or you can let it work against you. The choice is yours. It all depends on how patient, cautious, and intelligent you are with your placements from here.

CHAPTER 7

Double(s) Trouble

⚲ *THE DREADED LOB*

Nothing can disrupt a match, change its flow, or alter opponents' strategies more than a *lob* can. Many even view it as the single most dreaded shot in the game. But why? There are many shots which could be considered difficult to defend. Blazing serves, aggressive approach shots, big forehands, returns that dive at the feet . . . so why is a shot as simple as the lob so feared?

The threat of the lob is as much the killer as the lob itself to defenders at the net. Many fear it for several reasons: first, the overhead is a shot that few practice often enough. Players stroke countless forehands and backhands each practice, while the number of overhead hits can usually be counted on one hand! The result is little confidence and belief in their shot-making ability with the stroke. Second, players lack the understanding of how important backward mobility is at the net. To defend the lob requires quick retreat and exact positioning of the feet. Third, the sky is the backdrop for overhead shots. Players aren't used to judging balls played overhead and have trouble with perception. Finally, most try to play the shot as it's sometimes named — a *smash!* The outcome is inconsistent play which ultimately breeds lack of confidence in the overhead stroke.

While both their backhands share the center of the court, a lob down the middle has taken the aggressiveness away from Peter Fleming and John McEnroe. Notice how McEnroe moves to cover behind Fleming while he attempts to strike the ball.

♀ THE MOST EFFECTIVE SHOT IN DOUBLES

Teams that never lob allow their opponents to move in closer and take control of the net. Teams that lob with accuracy, on the other hand, can keep opponents at bay, off the net. They are able to gain the advantage by placing balls at their opponents' feet or by taking over the net themselves. Teams that lob well also keep the ball in play more often and offer opponents a chance to err. This is why the lob, when properly executed, is the most effective shot in doubles at every level.

Most doubles players will, however, shy away from using the lob. They feel that they will be labeled "lobbers," "pushers," "moonballers," and the like if they are seen lobbing very often. They never truly understand the importance of the lob or how they can better use it; they prefer to avoid it instead. Fear is another factor in not lobbing more often. These players have "popped" short balls up in the air before, only to have waiting opponents rip overheads either easily away or worse, directly at them or their partner. What is often lacking is the understanding of how to control the lob. They've simply missed too many in the past to continue confidently attempting the shot during match play.

Lobs should be stroked similar to groundstrokes. Anyone can hit a ball up into the air, however, accuracy and direction require practice. A target must first be imagined to direct the ball there with control. Pop-ups or short floating lobs occur when players stop their swings at contact or shortly thereafter. Punches and flicks at the ball with open racket faces (strings directed to the sky) will send the ball upward but with little control. What is lacking is the proper follow through. The follow through of the stroke allows the racket to continue moving through the hit and direct the ball in the process. When players shovel or push the ball with little or no follow through, weak shots and ineffective lobs result.

Disguise is the key to success with the lob. When lobs are made to appear as though they are normal forehands or backhands and then suddenly the ball clears the head of unprepared opponents, it often is the best surprise tactic available. To better disguise your lobs, strive to stroke the ball in the same manner as if it were a groundstroke, only *lift* the ball a little more on the follow through as your stroke finishes. This way your opponents will have difficulty reading or reacting to what shot you are about to hit. It will also make them quite insecure positioning themselves very close to the net in the future.

Lobs are excellent strokes to try on hard to handle shots. They also offer instant relief on shots which have pulled your team out of position. Disguised lobs also come in another form, lob *volleys*. A block lob, such as a lob volley, can be quite surprising when executed properly and will surely keep opponents off balance and guessing. A lob can be made before the ball bounces (a volley) by opening up the racket face and adjusting the angle and power of the swing to just clear the head of the unsuspecting opponents and still land within the boundaries of the court.

When opponents are intent on playing in a one up/one back position, the lob is an excellent tool to use to tire the baseline opponent. By successfully lobbing repeatedly corner to corner, over the net person's head, the baseliner is forced to run from side to side. This will not only cause your opponents to make more mistakes while on the run, but it can also force them to take positions on the court they're not entirely comfortable with, such as both playing up or back.

Often the best return for you and your partner is a *lob return*. If the net person is actively poaching or the server is successfully serving and volleying, a lob thrown up over the net person's head is certain to thwart their plans. Outdoors a lob gives opponents plenty of sun and sky to look at and wind to face in attempting to hit overheads. Indoors, opponents face the bright lights, steel beams, and light-colored ceilings.

The lob is an important shot for you and your partner to keep in mind when planning strategy. Instead of using it as a last resort shot, practice to make it a part of your everyday stroke repertoire. Let it help you become a more complete team. It might even become the most effective shot your team uses!

⚲ OFFENSIVE VS. DEFENSIVE

Lobs can either be categorized as *offensive* or *defensive* shots. What determines whether a lob is an offensive or a defensive play is the positioning of the players attempting to lob and the height of the arc in the lob.

Offensive lobs are hit by players in good position or in command of the point. They are usually played off of shorter balls which easily allow players to step in behind the shot and lift it over the net opponent's head. The height of the offensive lob is a lower trajectory which, when correctly played, just clears the outstretched racket of the surprised opponent. The time the offensive lob remains in the air is also shortened, prohibiting the net player from getting the opportunity to run it down and return it back. A lob hit with topspin offers that much more advantage. A topspin lob dips quickly after clearing the net person's head and runs away usually untouched. This is the reason it is called an offensive shot; it is used to take control of the point or even win it outright.

Defensive lobs, on the other hand, are used by players who find themselves in some form of trouble. The high arc and long hang time of the defensive lob allow players needed time to get back into position or regain control of the point. When players are pulled out of the court or jammed with difficult shots, the high lob is the intelligent shot to choose. Opponents will, in all probability, be able to have a play on the lob, but the most important thing is that no errors will be committed in the process. When players try to "blast" their way out of situations, unintelligent play results through repeated errors.

Weaker players normally use the lob only as a defensive tactic, however, even very good players often lack the knowledge of how to use lobs more effectively. To place lobs more offensively and therefore more effectively, bring the ball down lower by driving your racket through the ball instead of lifting it so much on your swing. It is important to realize that it is the racket *face* and *plane* of your swing path that direct the ball on the lob. To bring your lob down, aim at the top of the fence on the side of your opponents. This lower trajectory will prove quite difficult for your opponents to defend when correctly controlled over their heads.

⚲ YOUR OVERHEAD PROBLEMS — "PAT AND MIKE"

The best smashes are taken overhead with a fully outstretched arm at a comfortable distance in *front* of the body. The stroke is to be played similarly to the serve, with body weight properly positioned behind the ball with the swing becoming a natural throwing motion of the arm. Most of the troubles that players experience with the overhead stroke, however, come when the ball is played from *behind* the body. The shot becomes extremely difficult to execute from here. Little or no body parts are positioned to offer stability or force for the stroke; even the eyes have a difficult time keeping it in view once it clears the head. This is the reason that "Pat and Mike" (your two feet!) have a very important job to do — preventing the ball from getting behind you!

Poor footwork is the cause of most overhead problems. The majority of players who dislike the stroke are the very ones who continually try to *cheat* while practicing it. They'll begin by standing near the service line so they won't have to run backward to take the ball overhead. In a match, who is going to lob these same players when they are positioned so far back at the service line? No one! These players need to practice by standing in too *close*, crowding the net. Now they can practice moving backward quickly and reacting faster to better position themselves to play the ball overhead. *Running* is what these players need to practice. Beginning their stance at the service line in practice just proved it.

The key to better "Pat and Mike" performance is to *avoid moving with the ball.* Lower level players experience overhead difficulties because they haven't learned this secret. Their feet track high balls at a speed which either never gets them into the proper position or gets them there only in time to make rushed, uncontrolled swings at the ball.

Advanced players *move faster than the ball.* They anticipate where the ball should be played and move quickly to set up at this location. When quick preparation is practiced, players are then afforded the time to set, pause, and execute. Players with slower feet rush their strokes and make awkward arm adjustments to compensate for lack of good positioning. Advanced players with sound overheads make the adjustments with their *feet* and are ideally positioned on a regular basis to allow for comfortable hits.

Preparation for the overhead stroke begins with a shoulder turn. This is to properly align the body for its natural swing at the ball. The racket then prepares by going up and back behind the head in a "cocked" action ready to strike. The free arm (one without a racket) then becomes a guidance or aim arm to help sight the ball overhead. Now is when "Pat and Mike" come into the picture. Footwork must be made quickly by sidestepping backward to keep the ball at a comfortable distance in front of the body.

Through experience and practice, your feet will take you to the ideal position for better overhead shots. When you do practice overheads, remember not to cheat! Stand in close to the net so that you must practice running backwards quickly. Even though height can be an advantage to players at the net, some of the best overhead hitters I've ever known were short! They made up for their lack of size by developing better positioning with quicker feet. Try not to make positioning adjustments with your arm and swing, but rather let your feet be what positions you correctly each time and allows comfortable hits.

℞ SMILE WHEN YOU'RE LOBBED

As a doubles player, considerable time will usually be spent playing the net. To develop a sense of security in your ability to play the net, you need a dependable overhead stroke with which you feel confident. Without possessing a strong overhead, your confidence in playing the net will surely be less. Even though you may volley quite well, as soon as your opponents discover your overhead deficiencies you'll be destined to give up points when taking a position at the net.

In developing a sound doubles game, one of the most beneficial strokes you could ever possess is a confident overhead. With it you could change entire strategies the opposition could devise. We discussed earlier how important a stroke the lob is in doubles at every level. If you could eliminate or even limit your opponents' lobs you could in essence control which strokes they would have to play.

Your practices probably need to be adjusted to provide more time to develop your overhead stroke, but isn't it worth it? It could give your team yet another advantage. If every time the ball popped up on your side of the court and you hit an "automatic winner," would your opponents continue to lob you? If they were smart they wouldn't. If you and your partner both made your overheads so automatic that you felt like smiling and saying thank you each time you were lobbed, opponents would be forced to attempt difficult passing shots instead.

Sometimes players fear the lob not because of their overhead abilities but rather because of winning lob placements. If offensive lobs continue to go over your heads, it's only because you're letting them! It's no one's fault but your own. Make your approach shots and volleys deeper, to the weaker opponent or to the weaker stroke. If they continue to hit winning lobs over your heads, move back several steps to prevent them from continuing to score. Move back to your previous position at the net once the winning lobs have ceased. Force them to hit the shallow balls you prefer.

You can also develop your ability to *read* the lob better. Notice your opponents when they lob. Watch how they prepare their rackets, shoulders, and swing. You should be able to position yourself much quicker by simply anticipating the shot better. Smile when you're lobbed. You know that it's coming by reading it early, you've controlled where it will go by your placements and positioning, and it's an automatic point for your team since you've practiced it so much and have developed confidence in your overhead!

℘ SHORT TO SHORT, DEEP TO DEEP

Many club players remain erratic with their overhead shots. They may have discovered ball control and placement with their groundstrokes but not with their overhead. To them, the stroke is simply a "smash"! Little thought is given to direction and placement for this stroke, only sheer power. However, power without control is like first learning to drive in a car race . . . immediately you're in trouble! This is exactly what many players experience with their overheads. They're using power before control with disastrous results.

Just as with all shots in tennis, a target for the overhead must first be conceived in the mind in order to place the ball accurately, with direction and control. Lobs that are hit shallow or short should be angled off short with winning overhead placements. Deeper lobs, on the other hand, which require backing up to the service line and beyond, should be returned back deep overhead.

It's important to understand this rule of *short to short* and *deep to deep* placements for overhead shots. Short lobs are to be directed away from opponents. There is more court to hit into because of the angles created when closer to the net. Players should utilize this extra court and direct the ball where their opponents aren't on short lobs. Problems occur when players are more concerned with smashing the ball and forget to direct it away from opponents to end the point. The result is often longer rallies (as more balls tend to come back) or more mistakes being made due to the uncontrollable power being applied to the ball.

Deep lobs on the other hand require more precautionary care. The shot becomes a transition or set-up shot when taken midcourt due to the limited angles created. By placing the ball back deep, players can then better position themselves by moving back into a closer net position to attempt to end the point on the next shot. *Patience* is what is required for deeper lobs. Overheads from here are not easily hit for winners. The intelligent doubles shot is to hit it for consistency, to set up for the next shot which offers a higher percentage chance for success. Shy away from playing the hero by attempting to smash your way out of all predicaments.

It is best to play most lobs without a bounce. Opponents then have less time to react and prepare for your overhead shot. However, when a lob is very high or very deep, letting the ball bounce before striking it overhead is the wise choice. Even though this gives more time to opponents to prepare for and read the shot, the ball is easier to manage and control after it has bounced. It also allows more time to get ideally positioned behind the ball to make accurate placements.

℺ COMMUNICATION WOES

The lob is an excellent tactic to use to cause confusion. When the ball is hit up high in the air, players are sometimes hesitant and unsure who should be the one to take it. When players lack the understanding of communication and positioning for these shots, their lack of teamwork can be easily exposed by clever opponents.

When your team is faced with lobs, don't panic. You're not defeated unless you let the shot break your team down. Quickly *communicate* who is to take the ball. Preferably this should be done by the person whose head the ball is clearing. "Mine" should be yelled quickly by this person if he intends to take it. "Yours" should be instantly said if he is unable to make a good shot with it or if he feels his partner has a better chance at it.

This simple yours/mine verbal communication should eliminate most of the confusion lobs can bring to your team. Make it a habit to communicate quickly each time the ball is lifted up overhead on your side of the court. You and your partner will then have a clear understanding of who is to take each ball. Teams that have been playing together for many years and inherently know who will take each ball may not need to pay as much heed to this lesson; however, I've seen many experienced teams fail through communication woes. Just because a team has been together for a period of time does not necessarily mean that simple communication isn't important. Quite the contrary, it will always be important.

You and your partner may decide beforehand who is best suited to take different lobs. Balls down the center of the court, for example, may be best played by the ad court player who can play balls more easily with the forehand overhead stroke and all high balls might be taken by the better overhead hitter of the two. In any event, the best eliminator of confusion is communication.

Positioning problems occur when players forget to *move together* when covering all lobs. When one moves backward prepared to hit, the other should move ready to take the shot if the partner is unable to. Backing up the partner this way provides added insurance that the lob will always be covered. Players who move together will also find themselves better positioned and prepared to react to opponents' hits. By balancing the court, holes are closed off which usually are created when players move independently covering lobs. In positioning yourselves for retaliation of lobs, remember that moving together is what is required. Not only will your team get back more balls, but you'll also have a balanced court which offers a more formidable shield of defense.

THE FACTOR THAT OFTEN SEPARATES THE LEVEL OF PLAYERS

The ability to hit lobs and overheads effectively is what often separates the levels in doubles. These two important shots provide added depth to players' games. Those who have advanced to a higher level have done so by developing a well-rounded game they can rely on. They understand the importance of shot selection and have chosen not to limit theirs by neglecting to develop these two very important strokes.

When perfecting the lob, work to vary the heights and trajectories of your hits. This will help you learn to control the ball either offensively or defensively, whichever the situation requires. Attempt to lob the ball with disguise, much the same as if you were stroking a normal forehand or backhand. This is a good surprise tactic to help you gain control of the point. Once your disguised lob clears the opponents' heads, they are forced to turn and run backward for it. This is the ideal time to follow your lob into the net position and steal the offense away.

Overheads should be practiced more often to make them into reliable strokes. Remember that footwork is the key to proper alignment and comfortable hits. Adjustments should also be made in your hitting "up" on the ball to place the ball short or deep, hitting the sides of the ball to direct it either right or left. *Let your racket do the work* to add power to the stroke by accelerating it up and through the ball. Make your overhead swing smooth and flowing. Even though the stroke is called a smash, your best results will come through accurate placements that are consistent, not necessarily powerful.

⌕ *SUMMARY*

Most players fear the lob more than any other shot in the game. Even though this is the case, rarely do players try to understand the shot's effectiveness and develop it to be an important part of their doubles game. With disguise, the lob could become the most effective shot your team possesses. There is a difference between offensive and defensive lobbing. Understand that there is a time for each, depending on the shot played to you and the shot you are about to play. Get your feet moving for better overheads. Your feet will make the adjustments to line your body up for the hit, not your arm taking the ball at all different heights and locations.

Make your overhead into a dependable stroke and you'll be smiling when you're lobbed. Direct short lobs short and and deep lobs deep. The third item of importance in the three

P's of sound overhead hitting (Preparation, Positioning, Placement) is *placement*. Stay away from smashing your way out of all situations. Avoid the problem that lobbing can bring your team by communicating better with your partner. Move together to keep more balls in play and to balance the court for defense. To advance your level, develop a well-rounded game with controlled lobs that are both offensive and defensive and reliable overheads that can be directed both short and deep equally well.

CHAPTER 8

Movers, Poachers, and Shakers

⚲ THE NET PERSON CONTROLS THE POINT

Players positioned at the net can be in control of the point whether they are touching the ball or not. When in motion, active net players cause opponents to be distracted and even confused. They tease the receiver by dancing in place and stepping toward the center of the court either to intercept the ball with a volley or to fool them by faking such an attempt. Opponents make more mistakes than usual when they are forced to attempt shots they aren't comfortable with such as riskier shots that have a lower percentage chance of success.

Poachers are out to steal the shot at the net. They *poach* or move across the court into their partner's territory to "nab" the ball for a winning placement. The goal of the poacher is to win the point by putting the ball away. They attempt to poach for surprise and to put added pressure on opponents to produce more difficult, riskier shots closer to the lines and net in order to get the ball by them.

Poaching at the net is like playing "cat and mouse" with the receiver. The poacher is the cat, ready to pounce at the mouse (ball) trying to get by safely. The more active the cat is at the net, the more difficult it is for the mouse. If the cat chooses to be lazy though, and sleep while at the net, little threat is placed on the receiver and the mouse is able to creep by at any pace or angle desired.

To control the net, the poacher must be *active*. He instills doubt in the receiver by either poaching or faking to poach on

Betty Stove takes control of the point by aggressively poaching a backhand volley.

every hit. If the poacher cannot volley, obviously he will pose no threat to opponents. This is why it is first important to develop a reliable volley in order to function in control at the net. However, the beauty of the poach is that even if unsuccessful, it can still be an effective way to control future points. Opponents will remember how you darted across the court to poach the volley and even if you missed the shot, they will know you're capable of repeating the maneuver and will feel threatened. If their play for the remainder of the match could be adversely affected by an unsuccessful poach, think of how you could control their play if your poaches were successful!

⚲ READING YOUR OPPONENTS

Players at the net who have become good poachers have not done so by chance. They have developed their poaching into a skill with precise timing and movements. Through keen *intuition* and *perception,* they have learned when it is the right time to poach and when it isn't.

Artful poachers usually key their maneuvers off their opponents. They look for predictable returns or favorite shots to anticipate where the ball will be hit. They watch what opponents do with their rackets, shoulders, and body movements to direct the ball to different locations throughout the match. They are then able to move to the location on the court where the ball will be traveling before it actually gets there because they have effectively anticipated the shot.

Anticipation is often no more than instant recall of a previous situation. This is the time to turn your mind "on" and let it benefit your doubles play. Shots your opponents have made in various situations in the past are stored information in your computer mind. When these situations occur again, let your mind recall what happened before to better prepare you for the shots they will probably attempt.

To steal a base in baseball, intense concentration and focus on the pitcher are required of the base runner. Once the runner sees that the pitcher has committed to throw to the batter and home plate, then and only then can he attempt to steal. If the runner is unable to read the pitcher effectively, chances are he won't be successful in stealing. This is also true of poachers at the net in tennis. To steal the shot at the net, poachers must be able to read the opponent. Without a perceptive eye, players will certainly experience their share of poaching difficulties.

◌ *TIMING IS THE KEY*

Expert poachers not only read their opponents well, they also time their movements precisely. Ill-timed poachers often "send up a flare" to opponents signaling a poach is being attempted. This makes an easy mark for opponents to pass down the uncovered alley. Clever poachers, however, never let their opponents see them move. They have learned how to outsmart their opponents by perfecting their *timing*.

When players prepare their racket and feet to align properly for the stroke is the time they should be contemplating where the ball will be directed. Net players who leave too early on the poach make the decision an easy one for them. They simply direct the ball where "no one is home," down the line. Patient net players have better success at picking off returns. Waiting until the opponent has decided where to direct the ball (instead of deciding for them by going too early) will increase their chances for successful poaches.

Once a player has begun the forward swing of the racket on a stroke, he has committed to the shot. It is extremely difficult to change or alter the stroke at this instant. A wise poacher recognizes this and takes off *at the exact moment the opponent begins the forward swing*. The ball has not yet been struck by the opponent and yet the net player is able to "cheat" in his positioning by stealing several timely steps toward the center of the court in anticipation. By timing the movement, players are able to poach more balls and are able to do so without alerting opponents to their intentions.

◌ *AUTOMATIC POACHING TIMES*

Situations often occur during match play which offer terrific opportunities for net players to poach. Alert net players who recognize these situations will be able to make them become *automatic poaching times* and will surely profit from their intelligence.

High balls hit *to* opponents are usually quite difficult for them to handle, especially if they must stroke the ball from shoulder height or higher. This presents a golden opportunity for net players to poach. High balls hit *from* opponents also present opportunities. Balls that float up high without much pace should signal an automatic poach.

Low returns which require opponents to hit or volley "up" allow the net person an easier poach. To hit down the line over the highest part of the net is extremely difficult on these low balls, so opponents are forced to go crosscourt almost every time. Active net players see this as a situation to poach on and will do so automatically each time the ball is hit low to opponents.

Balls placed in the center of the court are an easier poach than balls played out wide. Wider balls require more coverage of the alleys thus prohibiting free movement at the net. Deep serves and shots force weaker replies as do shots hit harder with more pace. Advanced players quickly prepare to poach when these situations occur.

Once you and your partner recognize which shots your opponents dislike, it will then be easier for each of you to set the other up for the winning points at the net. The baseline partner hits lower, higher, deeper or harder shots, keeps the ball down the center of the court or to the opponents' weaknesses. The net partner is then able to play the hero by picking off easy volleys. This is when teamwork is so vitally important in doubles. Net players are able to win more points and influence the outcome of matches when their partners learn to help by setting them up better. Without help from their partner, net players are forced to remain less active and therefore less threatening while positioned at the net.

♀ FAKES AND DOUBLE FAKES

Net players who appear to be going after every ball can be very intimidating. They become "obstacles" opponents must attempt to hit around. It is an increasingly more difficult task to accomplish the more the net person moves. This is why active net players control the points they play, while passive net players merely watch the points played. When players poach every time, however, there is little guesswork on what will occur. Opponents simply wait for the net player to shoot across the court and then play the ball behind them for winners down their alley. Clever net players mix up their movements and their opponents. They don't allow opponents to get comfortable because they never let them know what they will do next.

The best net players *always move.* They don't always poach, but they do always move as if they were going to poach. By faking to poach and then staying sometimes, opponents see the movement at the net but are unsure of what will occur. It brings uncertainty into the opponents' minds, keeping them off balance and always uncomfortable with their play.

Players faking a poach make their movements before opponents begin the forward swing of the racket. Remember, once the forward swing of the racket begins, the player has committed to the shot. Fakes must occur *before* this commitment to make the opponent *think* they are going. He will then try to outwit the poacher by playing the shot down the alley. To his surprise, the net person didn't go at all but is instead waiting there for the ball to come right to him!

Double fakes are another clever maneuver that can keep your opponents confused. When opponents become wise to your fakes and poaches and are able to read when each will occur, throw them completely off by double faking or by faking and then going. Faking early while the stroke is being prepared and then once again just before she commits to make the shot, will bewilder your opponent. Faking and then going sometimes will completely secure control of the points by keeping your opponent perplexed and unable to read your intentions.

Players learning to fake must realize that unless their movements are seen, little threat will be felt by their opponents. Slight head, body, or foot movements may not be enough to cause attention or draw concern. The closer the ball is to opponents the more extreme the movements must be since their focus is keener on the ball.

All this going, faking, double faking, and faking and going can be tiring and certainly requires a lot more effort than simply standing motionless at the net. The results, however, will make all of your hard work worthwhile. You'll not only lose more calories at the net, you'll also win a lot more points!

♀ EVERYONE IS AFRAID OF A CRAZY PERSON

"Crazy people" are thought to be that way because they act irrationally. Because their reactions aren't normal, it's always difficult to figure out just what they will do next.

Everyone is afraid of a crazy person. Fear of them mostly centers around *uncertainty*. One never knows what to expect from someone who doesn't act normal. Hyperactive net players are feared in just the same manner. They are thought to be "crazed" up there at the net with all of their movements and because of this, opponents are fearful of them. The most effective net players in doubles, although thought to be crazy, are successful because they are mentally superior! They have realized how to alter and control their opponents' shot-making abilities through their actions at the net.

Active net players can cause confusion and teamwork troubles for their own team as well, unless adjustments are made to compensate for all of the movement. As a rule of thumb, players who poach across the center service line (which divides the length of the court in half) should stay on the side they have crossed into whether they've made contact with the ball or not. This will aid the deeper partner in realizing which side of the court to cover. He must switch to cover the territory left open by the net person. If the person runs back and forth in front of the net, the deeper partner is left in doubt as to which half of the court to cover.

⚲ *EVERY BALL IS COMING TO YOU*

Many players experience problems at the net because they lack intensity and readiness. They've assumed the net position but aren't actually prepared to volley. They're used to volleying only when the ball is directed to them and since this doesn't always occur in doubles, they're surprised when the ball does finally come in their direction. After they've made several mistakes at the net, they appear even less prepared to volley on future hits. Instead of sharpening their intensity to volley better, they resolve to guard their immediate area only by attempting fewer volleys since their confidence has been lowered.

The best way to prepare at the net is to think *every ball is coming to you*. In this manner, you will remain intense and ready to volley on each exchange. You need not *wait* for the ball to come to you, simply plan and prepare as if you will be volleying each ball played by your opponents. The best volleys will occur when you *go to the ball* instead of waiting for it. By thinking each shot will be directed for you to volley, your awareness and focus on the ball will be sharpened. It will also help you avoid the surprise when the ball finally does come your way.

♀ *OFFENSIVE/DEFENSIVE RULE*

When volleying, remember this simple rule: Balls that are taken higher than the level of the net are to be played offensively, while those taken lower than the net are defensive shots.

This is a very important rule to follow when playing close to the net. Balls that are higher than the net should be put away or hit for winners. They are to be angled off, hit between opponents, or hit directly *at* the closest opponent since his reaction time is shortest. Higher balls represent *opportunities.* They are the ones to play aggressively or offensively. Avoid blocking high volleys back to the deeper opponent who has more time to react to it. Players who neglect to take advantage of these high ball opportunities are committing tactical errors which can prove costly.

Another costly mistake which occurs even more often is when players hit lower volleys too aggressively. They attempt to hit winners on *all* volleys so the lower volley is treated the same as the higher one. The lower volley is, however, a more difficult shot since it must first clear the net. *Caution* must be used in executing it. Racket faces should be more opened at contact on the hit to allow better net clearance and depth on the shot. The entire body lowers for well controlled low volleys, not just the racket. Lower played balls, unlike higher ones, are to be directed *away* from the closest opponent.

Ideally, all balls are volleyed above the net level. Aggressive net players try not to allow the ball to drop below the top of the net. They quickly move either straight forward or at a slant to catch the ball early at its peak before it drops. They avoid moving parallel to the net across the court. They know how to take advantage of their positioning and play offensive shots at the net. They do, however, understand the offensive/defensive rule; they merely elect to play offensively at the net. They realize that as soon as the ball dips below the net the advantage shifts to their opponents, so they work on their quick forward movement. By taking the ball high they're able to play offensively and therefore retain control of more points played at the net.

♀ *WHAT ARE YOU WORRYING ABOUT — 4½ FEET?*

Most players net trouble stems from backward priorities. They are usually so concerned with covering their 4½ foot alley that they forget the remaining 31½ feet across the court! The shot to be concerned with in doubles is not the alley shot, it is (much to the surprise of most) the *crosscourt shot!* This shot offers the largest and safest target area to hit into and is the shot so often *given* to opponents.

How often do opponents direct the ball down your alley in doubles matches? The higher numbers of alley shots that your opponents must play, the higher level of player you probably are. Alley shots represent lower percentage play. The court is shorter, the angle is less, and the net is higher. These are the very shots you want your opponents to play! Make them hit down your alley more, don't give them the easy crosscourt shots.

The biggest problem with lower level players is that they stand too close to the alley. Their duty, they feel, is to cover that 4½ foot strip even though the ball will probably only come that direction several times in the entire match. They have their priorities backward. Their stance should begin in the center of the service box. With one huge cross-step and an outstretched racket, they should be able to adequately cover the entire alley barring several inches. By choosing a stance closer to the center of the court, opponents then have a smaller target crosscourt to hit into and are forced to consider the more difficult shot down the alley (which is already covered).

If opponents are only directing a few balls down your alley each match, you're probably not doing the best job at the net that you could. Make them hit the low percentage shots by taking away their high percentage safe crosscourt hits. Don't be afraid of shots to your alley, start being more concerned with routine crosscourt placements.

⚲ FROZEN DELIGHT

While one player prepares to strike the ball, the other three should avoid standing and watching without moving. Players at the net, especially, should be moving and positioning themselves constantly throughout the point.

Players who are frozen at the net like statues aren't imposing. This is where many matches can be decided. Holding and breaking serve has a great deal to do with the net person. What he does, how well he plays, and how much he forces are all important contributing factors in determining the outcome of each game. When the net person is idle, he's not likely to be an asset to the team. On the contrary, if he moves and volleys well and forces mistakes in the process, his team will probably experience its share of success no matter how strong his partner is.

When playing the net, move about to cause your opponents concern and to aid your partner. You will hold and break serve as a team and your efforts at the net can greatly influence the score. Get moving — don't be a "frozen delight" for your opponents to enjoy!

⚲ SUMMARY

To control the point from the net, players must be active. By moving more at the net, opponents are forced to try more difficult shots and will make more errors in the process. Intelligent poachers read their opponents to anticipate which shots they will hit. They time their movements precisely by waiting until the opponent has committed to the shot. They steal several crucial steps toward the center of the court before their opponent has struck the ball to better position for the volley. They are even alert to recognize times that call for automatic poaches. When these situations occur, they are primed to poach and learn to do so automatically. *Effective net players always move.* They don't always poach, but they do appear as if they are going each time. Their opponents are never able to get comfortable with their play because they're always more concerned with what the net person will do than what they're doing with the ball.

Prepare at the net with the intensity and readiness as if every ball is coming to you. It will help you avoid awful volley surprises. Remember the golden rule at the net: balls higher than the net are offensive shots while those taken lower than net level become defensive ones. Stop worrying about your alley and start worrying about the easy crosscourt hits your opponents keep making! Tempt your opponents instead to try your alley. The success of your team depends a great deal on what you do at the net, so make things happen by learning to control the court from there.

CHAPTER 9

Advancing
Through the Levels

⚲ GOING SOMEWHERE?

So . . . you and your partner are ready to make the big move. Both of you are primed to challenge and climb your way up the tennis ladder of success. But are you *both* committed to this quest? Undertaking such a journey solo usually causes friction and hardship among teammates. This is why it is important to establish *compatible goals* when teams wish to advance. Without a common understanding of where the team currently is and where the team wants to go, little thought is usually placed on trying to get there.

On every trip you've ever taken, you had a departure location and an arrival destination. You then set out on your journey to get there. If, however, you didn't know where you were or had no idea where you were going, do you think you would have had a successful trip?!

Unfortunately, this is the downfall of many tennis players and the very reason many drop from the sport. It's often difficult to figure just what your level in tennis is, much less pinpoint how to get to the next highest level.

Golfers have it easy. They have a handicap system in their sport. Not only is it easier to match up ability levels, it's also easier to define the levels in golf. If a golfer shoots an average of ten strokes over par (72) for eighteen holes, his handicap is ten. To improve, he must simply work at lowering his handicap score.

Tennis players have no handicap system to rate themselves. They label themselves as C, B, A, or Open level players, often unsure exactly which category best describes their play. Since these category levels vary according to city, state, and club, it makes it even more confusing to define what level their tennis game actually is. And when players have a difficult time figuring where they currently are, trying to get to a higher and again undefined level seems an impossible journey.

The United States Tennis Association in conjunction with the United States Professional Tennis Association and International Racquet Sports Association have adopted a tennis player rating system called the "National Tennis Rating Program" or NTRP System. Its aim is to provide a "simple, initial self-placement method of grouping individuals of similar ability levels . . ." The rating categories describe various skill levels in the game. Listed below are the NTRP skill levels. Read all the categories carefully and decide which category best describes your current personal ability level as well as that of your team.

To advance to the next highest level, simply read the higher categories to discover what you and your partner are lacking. Make sure each of you understands the higher category and you are willing to work together to advance your games to reach it.

NTRP RATING CATEGORIES

1.0 This player is just starting to play tennis.

1.5 This player has limited playing experience and is still working primarily on getting the ball over the net; has some knowledge of scoring but is not familiar with basic positions and procedures for singles and doubles play.

2.0 This player may have had some lessons but needs on-court experience; has obvious stroke weaknesses but is beginning to feel comfortable with singles and doubles play.

2.5 This player has more dependable strokes and is learning to judge where the ball is going; has weak court coverage or is often caught out of position, but is starting to keep the ball in play with other players of the same ability.

3.0 This player can place shots with moderate success; can sustain a rally of slow pace but is not comfortable with all strokes; lacks control when trying for power.

3.5 This player has achieved stroke dependability and direction on shots within reach, including forehand and backhand volleys, but still lacks depth and variety; seldom double faults and occasionally forces errors on the serve.

4.0 This player has dependable strokes on both forehand and backhand sides; has the ability to use a variety of shots including lobs, overheads, approach shots, and volleys; can place the first serve and force some errors; is seldom out of position in a doubles game.

4.5 This player has begun to master the use of power and spins; has sound footwork; can control depth of shots and is able to move opponent up and back; can hit first serves with power and accuracy and place the second serve; is able to rush the net with some success on serve in singles as well as doubles.

5.0 This player has good shot anticipation; frequently has an outstanding shot of exceptional consistency around which a game may be structured; can regularly hit winners or force errors off of short balls; can successfully execute lobs, drop shots, half volleys, and overhead smashes; has good depth and spin on most second serves.

5.5 This player is capable of being ranked at the sectional level; has developed power and/or consistency as a major weapon; can vary strategies and styles of play in a competitive situation.

6.0 This player typically has had intensive training for national tournament competition at the junior and collegiate levels and has obtained a sectional ranking.

6.5 This player has a reasonable chance at succeeding at the 7.0 level, has extensive satellite tournament experience, and has obtained a top collegiate ranking.

7.0 This is a world class player, any male currently ranked in the top 500 on the ATP computer and any woman ranked in the top 200 on the WTA computer. This player is committed to tournament competition on the international level and whose major source of income is tournament prize winnings.

ℚ WINNING ISN'T AS IMPORTANT AS LEARNING AND IMPROVING

Success, unfortunately, is often measured by wins and losses in tennis, like most sports. "Did you win?" is the first question from the mouths of parents, coaches, and friends to players after a match. Although winning does bring with it a sense of instant gratification, its effects stop there. To continue your ascent up through the levels, *learning* and *improving* are the most important factors. Without these two, your tennis game is left to stagnate, unable to progress even if you're winning. Let me explain.

To win and not learn from the match is a *win/loss*. Although a victory is recorded, the player has really lost because she hasn't progressed in the process. Players who continually score win/losses are certain to turn these to *loss/losses* in the future. When players reach a plateau with their game, this is exactly what has happened. They are unsure of how to progress because they have under-utilized their mental capabilities to help them reach their potential best by neglecting to learn from the matches they've played.

Losing a match but learning in the process can make the outcome easier to swallow. When players learn the reason for their losses, discover which strokes need attention, and formulate better strategies against their opponents, they have scored a *loss/win*. Even if the score was lopsided, the losing player has obtained from the experience a wealth of knowledge necessary to advance, so actually the player has really *won* from the match! To win the match *and* learn in the process is ideal, however, when players strive to learn from each outing on the court whether the score indicates a win or loss, they are guaranteed to continue improving their tennis games.

Be specific in search of the answers from the match or practice you've played. Replay the key points in your mind, search for the good and bad shots your team played as well as those of your opponents. Try to recall when the momentum of the match changed and what caused it to do so. Attempt to remember your thoughts as well. Discuss as many aspects of the match as possible with your partner following its conclusion, whether you won or lost. The two of you will then be gaining valuable insight from the experience. It will also help each of you better analyze occurrences *during* matches, thus enabling your team to score many victories through your intelligence.

Educators understand that for knowledge to "stick" or remain in the mind, it must be used and practiced. Players who are trying to advance through the levels must put their learned knowledge to the test and use it on the court. Challenge the teams that have been difficult to play well against in the past, don't avoid them. Compete against *all levels* of players to learn how to play best against each. Put your team to the test. Compete in tournaments when you get the opportunity. It might prove to be the least expensive lesson you've ever had! Search for the way to continue learning and share newfound knowledge with your partner. Your team will never waver from the path of improvement when its primary focus is on learning, whether the scores you record are favorable or not.

ℚ *THE MENTAL EDGE*

Tennis is very much a mental game. It is extremely difficult, however, to say exactly what percentage of the requirements is mental and what percentage is physical for the players. As the level of play rises, the importance of the mental requirements is certainly that much more increased.

Experienced players have their minds in control. They are *concentrated* or in focus, allowing for maximum mental potential. They also have their minds turned "on" to strategic and tactical thinking to avoid mindless play. They have belief and confidence in themselves by choosing positive thoughts to describe their play.

To play equally well against all levels requires a high state of concentration. It's often easier to play well and concentrate better against tougher opponents than it is when playing easier matches. Minds tend to wander out of boredom or lack of intensity against lesser opponents. However, to develop your minds (and your games), optimum concentration should be your goal every time you take to the courts. It shouldn't matter whether it's practice, a lesson, a club match, tournament play, or just a hit. You will get back from your mind what you allow it to do. Attempting to focus in on your play sporadically will usually result in inconsistent or sporadic play. Consistent winning players who have successfully advanced their games have all learned to concentrate on every hit *no matter who is on the other side of the net.* They have discovered the secret of playing well consistently — consistently concentrating!

Players who are mentally prepared and ready for the matches they play don't *react* while playing, they *act.* Those who react to situations on the court haven't given much thought to them, while the players who act have the foresight to develop a plan for what they will do. With this in mind, they are able to follow out their plan with their actions on court.

Strategic and tactical planning comes about through *habitual thinking*. Better thinkers in tennis, however, usually aren't made overnight, they are developed over time. Generally, the higher the level of player, the better they are at spotting weaknesses. This is why many past playing professionals are able to make the transition to the teaching courts. They have advanced in the sport by learning how to read their opponents. On the teaching court, they will continue to spot weaknesses across the net, only this time they will be helping others, not exploiting them!

To become better thinkers, analyze your own games as well as those of your opponents. Tailor your strategies to suit your styles of play and the game necessary to play against your opponents. This game plan is contingent on your opponents and their weaknesses.

Q. *Who has the weaker overhead?*
A. Lob this person.

Q. *Is one opponent weak in returning serves?*
A. Poach more against this person.

Q. *Does either have a weak second serve?*
A. Stand in and take advantage of it.

Q. *Which opponent is the weaker volleyer?*
A. Play this person at the net.

Q. *Is one person slower?*
A. Play this person more out wide.

Q. *Which are their favorite strokes?*
A. Play all others, not these.

Q. *What are their favorite positions on court?*
A. Make them play other positions.

Q. *What is the weakest stroke they possess?*
A. Play this one, time and time again.

Q. *At what height do they prefer to take shots?*
A. Give them all other heights.

Q. *What pace do they prefer?*
A. Play shots to them at the pace they don't like.

Be flexible in your planning after their weaknesses have been analyzed and discussed. Situations are known to change during match play. A weakness played over and over again can become grooved and actually turn into a strength as the match progresses. You must take notice of these changes and be prepared to adapt new strategies when they occur.

Your tennis game will only advance to the level you think it can. It sounds simple, but it's very true. Positive thinking is controlled thinking. Few things can be achieved without it. Let negative or doubtful thoughts enter your mind and they begin to consume your belief and determination, eventually holding you back from your quest. Be careful in choosing your thoughts. Discipline yourself to think positive thoughts both on and off the court to help build confidence and belief in your game. Your mind will help take you to great heights or it will hold you from reaching them. The choice is yours, since only you are in control of your mind!

℺ *THE STROKES TO TAKE YOU THERE*

Doubles is a game requiring consistent strokes along with percentage placements. Retrievers, however, who neglect to take advantage of court positioning and effective shot selection will struggle with the advancement of their games. This is because it is important to understand that as the level of players increases, the purpose and quality of the placements improve. Balls can't simply be hit back over the net any longer, they must be accurately directed for optimum results.

The primary focus for your team should be to win your serves. The easier it is for your team to hold your serves, the easier it will be for your team to advance. It sounds frightfully simple, however, it should be the very basis your team builds its game on. HOLD SERVE! Work with your partner at holding serve more easily. The strokes that will take you there are a high percentage *first serve* and a *reliable (and quality) second serve.* Servers must learn to make opponents "work" through accurate placements. Receivers shouldn't be comfortable returning the ball by simply standing, turning, and hitting. Servers must aim for the corners of the service box and force the receiver to lunge, stretch, or run in attempting the return. He should alter, change, or mix up the serve so the opponents never feel comfortable knowing what to expect. Balls hit with varying spins accomplish this as do strokes which vary the speed and placement of the hit to keep opponents guessing. Clever servers exploit opponents' weaknesses and mix up their delivery enough to throw off the rhythm and timing most receivers crave.

To hold or win serve requires a team effort. Without help from the net partner, the server will have his share of trouble attempting to win the game alone. The strokes that count here are the *volley* and the *overhead.* If there is an opportunity to put the ball away, the cardinal rule for the net person is to do just that, *put it away!* Net players should be on the lookout for ways to help the team hold serve. Strategic advice and lots of movement and activity certainly help the cause, however, well-timed poaches and accurately placed strokes will ensure the team's success.

Breaking (or winning) opponents' service games is the other primary focus for your team. The important strokes for breaking serve are the *return of serve, lob,* and *volley.* Successful returners direct their shots with consistent control. They stay away from low percentage shots that produce inconsistent results. While the crosscourt return is the percentage play, receivers must work to keep the ball in play effectively and at the same time away from the offensive grasp of the serving team. Low dipping returns or deeper placed lobs can be used to thwart the serving team's offensive plans. Once the offense has shifted away from the serving team with such placements, the receivers should strive to take advantage of the situation by stealing the offensive position away. Control of the point then shifts to the receiving team.

Holding and breaking serve can only be accomplished with consistent and reliable strokes. Obviously, it's very difficult to move to the next highest level with glaring stroke weaknesses. You need strokes you can depend on. The five strokes discussed — the serve, volley, overhead, return, and lob — are the basics necessary to accomplish the vital functions of holding and breaking serve. The more consistently accurate these strokes become, the easier it will be for your team to move up the ladder of levels.

♀ *DEVELOPING A BAG OF TRICKS*

Good politicians never seem to be at a loss for words. They can usually talk their way out of most situations, often clouding the issues with rhetorical jargon. They can take a question, give it no answer, and in the process lay the blame on their opponent! They seem to possess an uncanny knack for weaseling their way out of the issues. Successful doubles teams also come equipped with a "bag of tricks." They don't play the game unprepared, they appear to have answers for every situation long before they're ever faced with it. They are also clever in their reply, often keeping opponents off balance in the process.

A bag of tricks is nothing more than pre-programmed preparation. With careful review of the questions before they're ever asked, the answers always come easy. Likewise, by preparing your shot selection for the various situations your team will encounter, you will have a reply prepared and ready to answer during match play. What is required is a total game commitment from you and your partner. The team with the larger arsenal of tricks rarely finds themselves at a loss for match solutions, while teams whose bag of tricks is limited will discover only limited success with fewer replies.

"One-dimensional" players usually perform well at a single task. Maybe they play the game solely offensively or defensively, from only the baseline or at the net, or only with hard or soft shots. One-dimensional players will defeat some players but surely not all. They lack the total skills required to defeat a variety of styles and ability levels. They must become more well rounded as players to progress. Their bag of tricks needs to grow to score consistently well against the wide variety of opponents they will face.

Shot selection is a good starting place in the development of a total game. Even though good doubles should begin with a limited number of strokes you can count on, advanced doubles play requires a good working knowledge of *all the strokes.* Players who understand and have practiced a wide variety of hits will find themselves prepared to repeat these same shots in matches. Shots such as the drop shot, drop volley, lob volley, half volley, chip shot, approach shot, and shots played behind the head among others should be learned and developed. Quality of control, in spins, depth, and power, should also begin to be applied to the strokes you already possess to enhance their performance. Remember, building a larger arsenal of strokes can mean more answers in your bag of tricks to bring about more success for your team.

Developing a wider array of strategic plans can also increase your team's chances of success. Changing the positions your team plays when necessary — back for defensive maneuvers, up to the net for offensive plays, and creating new positions such as Australian doubles formation — keeps your team adaptable to allow for strategic changes. Developing a lobbing game, an attack game, a steady game, and a patient one can also best prepare you for these demands when the situation arises.

Finally, better control of the ball and its placement is vital in the advancement of your games. Those who have the ability to direct the ball both deep and short on all shots, high or low, and can hit the ball equally well hard or soft are able to place the ball effectively during a variety of match situations.

♀ HOW TO GET LUCKY

You and your partner will make your own luck in life. You will set yourselves up for it or not. You see, the harder you work in life, the luckier you will be!

Non-achievers refuse to believe this. They live their lives assuming luck is a chance happening that never seems to turn their way. Others' successes are rationalized purely in terms of luck, as they are jealous when others experience good fortune. They could probably find themselves much luckier in life if they learned simply to get down to work for it!

Unfortunately, there are very few shortcuts on the road to success. To have your "doubles cake and eat it too" will take work on the court, maybe even lots of it. Discipline is what will be required from you and your partner along with a high level of desire from you both. Once you decide to advance your level, commit yourselves to it by doing something more about it. Simply wishing or dreaming of improving will score your team as much success as that of a lottery–one out of several million chances of success!

Teams that prefer to practice by only playing matches together could discover more rapid improvement by altering their practice schedule. Training and drilling are necessary requirements in addition to match play. It is confidence and belief in strokes and selves that must be developed and this can often only be accomplished through repetitive practice. To improve, some teams need to simply *drill, drill, drill.* Practicing in this manner can be fun, a real challenge, or it can be a real bore. It all depends on the *attitude* of the team and the importance placed on improvement. How badly do the two of you really want to raise your level? If you want to enough, prepare yourselves to work for it.

Maybe you and your partner discover that the problem with your team lies in stroking deficiencies. If you're unsure of the problems, a lesson together with a qualified teaching professional might cure the ailment. However, if you are aware of the problem areas, use your practice time wisely. Maybe it's a single stroke such as your serve that needs attention. Place targets in the corners of the service boxes across the net and proceed along with your partner to direct several hundred serves to practice accurate placements. This is the way to improve your strokes. Focus in on the problem areas and then work together with your partner to develop confidence and belief in your strokes.

Practice the way you would like your team to play. If you and your partner are longing to become better serve and volleyers for example, spend more time in practice working on this game style. Your team will never serve and volley in important matches if you're not confident in doing it, so practice serving and volleying to develop your level of confidence to the point where you will feel comfortable using it in match play. Invariably, the way your team practices will dictate the way it will eventually play. If there is a stroke, strategy, or game style your team desires, simply spend more practice time developing your confidence in it.

When you and your partner have made an inner commitment to excel, your practices will have a *purpose.* They will become more challenging and rewarding once the importance is placed on improving in practice. Focus in on your practice time and prepare to *work* if necessary. Successful people have always attested to the fact that it wasn't reaching the top that brought them the most joy, but all the hard work and struggles along the way which were most rewarding. *Enjoy the challenge* and you and your partner will certainly become all the luckier for it.

♀ *DON'T FORGET: DOUBLES IS ANAEROBIC*

Those of you who think you're getting into shape while playing doubles, I've got news for you . . . doubles is an anaerobic exercise! What this means is, if you want to play top level doubles, you will have to get into shape through other means than just playing doubles. Having a fit body will bring not only physical benefits to yourself and your team, it will bring many mental benefits as well. For you and your partner to play your best, a commitment is required that each of you first get into the best shape that you can.

An aerobic base can be built in each of you through occasional singles play, running, walking, bicycling, aerobic class participation, or other exercises which include prolonged periods of constant movement and use between 60% and 90% of your heart's maximum reserve. Players who possess solid aerobic foundations recover more quickly and tire less often. They also usually have lower blood pressure, better stress levels, lower cholesterol levels, their weight more under control, and higher self esteem, not to mention play better tennis.

The reason singles is generally considered aerobic exercise and doubles isn't is due to the "work-rest" ratio in each. Doubles players have a shorter work-to-rest ratio than singles players who must cover the entire court themselves as well as strike every ball played to their side. Doubles played at the highest level is the exception to this rule. Most doubles, however, isn't played with enough effort to stir the cardiovascular system to significantly increase the body's oxygen intake. Doubles usually only produces about half the benefits of singles play and other such aerobic activities. This is the reason that doubles isn't considered a "fitness activity" by most sports medicine experts.

Advanced players recognize this fact and train in other ways to help benefit their doubles play. Are you and your partner in shape? If so, you're probably doing a combination of aerobic training along with playing doubles. If you don't feel that you're in the best of shape, I strongly urge you to supplement your doubles play with one or several fitness activities to better condition and prepare yourselves for optimum results.

⚲ SUMMARY

To advance your game, you and your partner need to assess where you currently are and where you would like to be in the future. Rate yourselves according to the NTRP scale to determine the level at which you play the game, then read the higher levels to ascertain what is needed to advance your games to these higher levels. Strive always to "win" from matches you play by constantly learning to improve. Even if your outcome scores are unfavorable, your team will stay on the road to success when you continually gain knowledge from every match you play. Players who win but don't learn in the process are really the true losers in the matches they play!

To gain the mental edge requires a mind in concentrated focus, strategic and tactical thinking, as well as belief and confidence through positive thoughts. It should make no difference who is on the other side of the net, the mental game is played within your head and only you are in control of it. The primary focus for you and your partner should be to *hold serve always* and *break serve whenever possible.* The strokes to take you there should be played with consistency for them to become reliable. Advanced doubles play requires, however, a broader scope of strokes, strategies, and control. Lower level players have limited successes since they remain limited in abilities, while advanced teams readily excel with a larger bag of tricks. If you and your partner want to get lucky, get down to work! The harder you work on the practice court, the luckier doubles team you'll become! If you're not in good shape, don't expect to improve your condition through doubles play. To play your best will require building a solid aerobic foundation through additional aerobic fitness activities. Get in shape to play your best doubles; don't assume your best doubles play will come about without it.

CHAPTER 10

Divorce Court Doubles

♀ BRINGING OUT THE BEST (OR WORST) IN YOUR PARTNER

Mixed doubles is fast becoming one of the most popular forms of tennis played today, especially at the club level. It offers the opportunity for men and women to compete together in a sport, often on equal terms. Although this chapter is mainly devoted to the game of mixed doubles, it really concerns "partnership troubles" which could equally be applied to men's and women's doubles as well.

The same basic winning attitudes apply to mixed doubles as they do for other doubles play. However, in mixed doubles additional mental pressures make the game a more difficult struggle for many. The female sometime feels inferior or even embarrassed if she is not able to do her part for the team. The male believes his role is the dominant one and will play with lower self esteem if he's not proving himself as the superior one on the court.

The way to bring out the best in your partner, no matter the gender, is to *instill confidence in them.* Make them feel *important* and show them *respect.* That is the best way possible to treat your partner. Everyone has at one time or another felt inferior or insecure on the tennis court. It is the *partner's duty* to help restore lost confidence. When tennis games are faltering, chances are players' confidence is as well. Players who understand this try to build their partner's confidence to help keep them sharp and playing their best. They make the best use of their partner's abilities by finding something to *compliment* them on. They may have to search for it on days their mate is playing poorly, but they are always looking for something their partner is doing "right" and share this with them. Remember, false flattery never works. Never has and never will, so don't try it!

Some partners insist on being the boisterous coach of the team, in charge of the court. If you are the sergeant of your team, learn to tone down your commands! No one likes to be judged or bossed around the court. Tactfully refrain from giving orders to your partner. Her performance will invariably be related to how well you can control your tongue.

If you are the one on the receiving end of such orders, make the effort to go along with the strategy or game plan your partner has devised. Compromise on little differences of opinion. Be willing to assume a submissive role if necessary to appease your high ranking partner and bring harmony to the team. Don't attempt to win "your rights as an equal partner" on the tennis court; save it for later off-court discussions.

When all else fails, remember this simple rule: *Keep it positive with yourself and your partner.* It's easy to allow negative thoughts to enter when all is going against you, but teams that have learned to trust in the positive regularly play better. Don't dwell on the little things that have happened on the court, the silly errors or missed shots. Try to focus on the good shots to put hope and optimism back into your thoughts. Stay away from criticizing your mate for mistakes or comparing him unfavorably to others. How you treat each other on the court (especially married couple mixed doubles teams) is often a good indication of just how well you actually get along.

℞ SWITCH RATHER THAN FIGHT

Your normally reliable partner has just hit his backhand into the net for the twenty-third time today, if anyone is counting. You're ready to scream, take his head off, or even disown him. There's one tiny problem...he's your husband!

Husband and wife teams must be extremely careful when playing on the same team. The problem is that the better you know someone, the less likely you are to mind your manners and watch what you say under stress. Since most tennis play is filled with stressful situations, couples unable to control their emotions are certain to feud on the tennis court. Those who have a tendency to become annoyed at their spouses' weaknesses, mistakes, bad habits, or personality might be setting themselves up for a "round in the ring" with their mate on the doubles court!

Most problems occur when players take their frustrations out on each other. Even though these players might just be letting off steam, the results to the team can be devastating! Spouses feel belittled and defensive, the team is pulled apart, and the problem still isn't solved! Instead of taking tension out on your partner, relax, get control of yourself, and *look for the answers* instead. What exactly is causing your team's hardships? Are you using the wrong strategy or game plan? Are you using the best shot selections? Is your team best positioned on the court? Discuss these and other ways to get back on track. That's what sensible players do. Senseless players remain more concerned with letting off steam than correcting the problems.

If you insist on playing to win, make sure your partner agrees and is willing to play that game as well. Others may not enjoy the game if you "hog" the court and smash balls at the opposing team to win points. In highly competitive situations your aim will be to expose opponents' weaknesses, but this can still be accomplished with good sportsmanship, integrity, and class.

Mixed level partnerships require each to understand the role they are to play on their team. The stronger player should take more balls, cover more of the court, and put more shots away to win the points. Weaker players should attempt to lob more, especially if they can place the ball high and deep with accuracy. It is important to understand each player's role if they are to play compatibly together. When these roles are reversed and problems arise with the team, it's not time to fight but rather to talk strategically.

Trading sides with your partner could be a wise move if the previous set played was a disaster. Maybe your opponents were placing the ball to your team's weaknesses with ease. Sometimes by changing sides you're better positioned to protect your weaknesses and play your strengths. It can also throw your opponents off if they've become grooved to particular placements that were once successful but no longer are.

Husbands and wives who enjoy the game of mixed doubles (but only as long as they're not playing as a team) can still play together on opposite sides of the court. By choosing a different playing partner but remaining on the same court with your spouse, you'll be able to experience mixed doubles matches together while staying married to each other.

Players who can laugh together, usually stay together and pose no breakup threat. If you're able to laugh, smile, and enjoy the game together, chances are you're playing with the right partner. If, however, you experience tense moments on the court, wanting to "kill" your partner, learn to take control of your emotions or make a partner switch. If you're not able to control your emotions with this partner though, are you sure you will be able to with another?

℞ SHOULD YOU ASK FOR A SEPARATION?

When your partner plays poorly, it can be a very helpless feeling. It is, however, important to remember that the day may come when your partner will have to carry you, so try to be understanding when your partner's play is down. Still, strained relationships can develop when players feel uncomfortable playing together. Maybe one player falls into a slump for a period of time, or the team has an unsuccessful streak, or something else has happened that affects the relationship of the partners.

Partnerships on the court are just like partnerships in life. A lot of learning, feeling, understanding, and effort are required to make it last. If staleness creeps in from routine, dull, or uneventful time spent together, *get creative!* To make a relationship work sometimes you may need to bring it out of boredom by making things more challenging and exciting. Make your time spent on the court more enjoyable with your partner. Bring back the zest that probably brought you two together on the tennis court to begin with.

Tension can be created by overreacting to the littlest things on the court. The sighs, looks, or courtesy extended to partners when they have missed a shot or made a mistake are crucial not only to their confidence but also to their dedication to the team. If you and your partner ever experience differences, the way you treat each other over the little things will be vitally important. Try to understand and settle your differences when they occur; don't be too quick to remedy the problem with a separation.

When all else has failed, a trial separation may be the answer. Separations provide needed time away and allow each some breathing room to evaluate the situation and sort things out. Players might just want to play with several other partners to see if a better partnership could be formed elsewhere. If successful, separations can provide the inspiration for partners to get together again "fresh" or the opportunity to recognize their incompatibility.

What is usually lacking in players who experience periods of poor play together is the *understanding* of what is causing them to play this way. Interaction differences are usually the result of poor play, not the cause. If, along with your partner, you've attempted to discover the reasons for your sub-par performance or you've uncovered them but are unable to find the cure, you might want to avoid a separation by taking one or several tennis lessons (together) with a local certified teaching professional.

♀ VISIT A MARRIAGE COUNSELOR (LOCAL PRO)

Teaching professionals sometimes have to assume the roles of psychologists and marriage counselors on the tennis court. Their paid advice helps not only to cure students' stroke mechanics, but their mental disturbances, problems in life, and partnership woes as well.

Just because I am a teaching professional does not mean that I endorse tennis professionals as "gurus" for all of life's problems! They can, however, help teams settle their differences or get their games back on track with sound, knowledgeable advice. They are available to instruct and guide teams with an objective eye and listen and counsel teams with an objective ear.

When partnership troubles begin, nip them in the bud with a lesson before they reach an uncontrollable stage. Taking lessons together can provide your team with the needed time to discuss strategies with a professional coach, discover and improve problem areas, settle little differences, or simply get you two back working together as *one*.

℞ LET THE EGO SLIDE

Mixed doubles, or "mixed troubles" as it's sometimes called, can be played just like any other doubles. What makes this game unique at times is the effect it has on one's *ego*. When both male and female compete together on the same court, the players can become overly concerned with what others on the court may be thinking of them (even more so than in regular doubles). What often results is some players trying to avoid appearing inferior by using harder hit strokes and more difficult shots than are necessarily required.

Macho guys who try to do it all usually end up losing it for the team (although they'll often blame their partner). These men shouldn't be so concerned with expressing their masculinity on the court, showing force and power in all their strokes. Important shots like lobs, touch, change of pace, and angles shouldn't be avoided in fear of losing masculinity. Full power on all hits is only successful in doubles at the highest professional level. Power pays off, but only when complete control is present.

Players must learn to rid themselves of ego concerns if they ever want to experience good doubles play. Self-centered players aren't concerned for the team, they're too interested in themselves. They tend to overplay shots and are willing to take wild gambles to end points too early. Players with healthy-sized egos are always looking for opportunities to "feed" their egos and keep them happy. To play this game well, these players must learn that the mixed doubles court will not be the time or place to nourish an ego.

Friends won't be won and partners can be lost when players act more in self interest than in the interest of the team. In social circles they certainly won't be viewed as gentlemen or ladies if they continually drill lesser opponents or try to win by knocking out the teams they play. Better ball control is what wins admirers, not harder shots. Better doubles players *use control to gain respect, not force to demand it!*

✑ THE IMPORTANCE OF A GOOD TALK

As with most relationships, doubles teams have a history of falling apart when there is a lack of communication present. Some people just prefer to keep more things in and only bring them out for discussion after they've been provoked or the number of items they've amassed reaches its peak. Others, who talk too much, lack communication skills as well since they neglect to *listen* well enough. Teams will, however, need to talk openly with one another no matter what personality traits they may have. They will need to discuss strategies as well as talk out problems. This is the reason that *communication* is so vitally important for any partnership to exist harmoniously for a length of time.

To become an effective communicator, remember that it's not always *what* you say, but *how* you say it that matters most. The tone you use in getting your point across might be the deciding factor in just how your point is taken. Your partner could become defensive if what you're trying to say is said "incorrectly" even if the message is a positive one.

During your talks, if you must give advice, make it helpful, not analytical or judgmental. When calling attention to a mistake, do so indirectly to avoid arousing resentment. Talk about your own mistakes first or begin with praise to make your partner happy to hear what it is you are about to say.

Good partners understand they must be willing to "give" as much as they are prepared to "take" in a relationship. They are good communicators because they are able to talk out their concerns effectively and listen sympathetically when the other has an idea to share. They don't set out to change their partner as much as to understand her. When communicating they use *tact* and *courtesy* and, above all, avoid nagging. They give honest appreciation during discussion, even for the smallest things. It's amazing how the problems these teams will experience can be worked out so easily when good communication skills are applied!

✑ NO ONE WINS AN ARGUMENT

The best way to win an argument with your partner is simply to avoid one! You may be completely right but as far as changing the other's mind or convincing them that you are right, you will fail just as if you were totally wrong.

When problems persist to the point of argument in a relationship, it's time for you to assess your interest in the team. Are you concerned about immediate or short-term gain or are you more interested in the long-term relationship of your team? This is an important consideration. Is your point worth risking your team? Not all arguments will break a team up, but since no one wins from an argument, certainly negative emotions challenge the stability of any pair.

Some situations are simply "no win" and partners must be able to recognize and deal with them intelligently when they occur. What they should strive for instead are "win-win" situations. This is when one player wins the other over to his side without demanding it. While communication skills remain important to achieving this task, so do negotiating techniques. Attempts should be made to see things from the other's point of view. This is probably the best way to truly understand people and their problems. Solutions must be thought out rationally and presented in a way to suit both of you. If the idea is yours, you might even need to let your partner think it was his. Don't always try to prove you are right, and if you're wrong, be the first to admit it.

Once you have learned to take the time to understand your partner and his problems, you will become more compatible with this person. Everyone acts as they do for a reason and your understanding of this reason will surely help you better understand the person and the problem. Coping with them in various situations will then become an easier task.

If your partner happens to behave irritably on court, take the time to understand what he may be going through. Don't lose your temper and fight at his time of need. Maybe varying moods are provoking such behavior. Possibly he is playing below normal standards because of other thoughts on his mind or happenings in his life. Be compassionate with your partner's needs. People often reveal their innermost selves on the tennis court. If your partner is at a low time, recognize that he might need your help. Don't kick him while he's down by provoking an argument.

Everyone loves a winner and that does not necessarily mean winners as indicated by the score. You will always be a winner by avoiding argument with your partner and a loser as soon as you enter into one!

ℚ *SUMMARY*

Instill confidence in your partner to bring out their best. Show them respect and make them feel important. It is often YOU who will bring out the best or worst in your partner. Avoid negative remarks to your partner as they only create negative performances. Sensible players look for and discover the reasons for poor play. They strategically talk when problems arise; they don't bicker and fight. Players who can laugh together will usually stay together. Don't be so quick to remedy the problems of your team with a separation. Try to understand and settle your differences. Interaction differences are usually the result of poor play, not the cause. Search for the true reason your team is faltering. Lessons together with a qualified teaching professional might provide helpful answers. Shed your ego concerns on the mixed doubles court. Play the game for the team, not for yourself!

Communication is the key to keeping teams intact. Remember that how you say something is as important as what you say. Use tact and courtesy while interacting with your partner. You'll probably discover that the problems of your team will be worked out easily when good communication skills are applied. Everyone wins an argument when one is avoided. Try to understand your partner better and see things from his point of view. Win your partner over to your way of thinking and learn to do so without demanding it.

CHAPTER 11

Double the Fun

℃ GETTING MORE ENJOYMENT FROM YOUR GAME

Why do you play the game of doubles? Have you ever asked yourself this question? There could be a thousand reasons for playing this game but the only important ones concern *your* reasons for playing it. Think on them for a moment. They can play an important part in helping you gain more enjoyment from your doubles play.

People generally tend to enjoy what they are good at, and the same can be said of tennis players. This doesn't necessarily mean you will proportionately enjoy the game more the better you play. I've seen a number of tennis "hackers" crazy about the game and some top-ranked ones who could easily give up the sport. What is important is what brings *you* the most enjoyment from playing doubles. Is hitting several "super shots" in matches what you enjoy most? Is improving your game and playing better doubles what you really crave? What about when you find the right partner and everything just seems to "click" on a given day. Is this what you enjoy most? Or is exercise and working out what you and your body need? How about the stresses and pressures of your everyday life? Is a game of doubles your escape? Only you have the answers to what brings you the most enjoyment from your game.

If you are like most, discovering and bringing out your best play is what is rewarding and exhilarating. But how often does this occur? If it's not very often it becomes frustrating to play continually at sub-par performance levels. Ambitious players in search of a higher level need to concentrate and "focus" more often while playing. To reach your potential consistently requires a commitment to excel along with a great deal of self discipline to continually perform at your peak. Mental, emotional, and physical demands are placed on you during play, and your ability to play well consistently is determined to a large extent on how well conditioned and prepared you are to handle these demands. Playing the game well does bring with it satisfaction and pride, however, it's often the hard work in the development of your game which is the most rewarding.

Don't allow frustrations to bring you and your game down. Pick yourself back up by focusing your mental energies on your play. RELAX and CONCENTRATE on what is occurring and above all, remain POSITIVE. Your controlled mental state will help to maximize your potential for optimum play. If this is what you truly enjoy, prepare to bring out your best. Don't expect it to come on its own; you will be frustrated when it doesn't.

℺ CHALLENGING YOURSELF TO BETTER DOUBLES PLAY

"Success is never final. Failure is never fatal. It is courage that counts . . ." Winston Churchill

Your doubles game is currently in one of three states: 1) improving; 2) on a plateau — showing no improvement but also no regression; 3) regressing. Into which category does your doubles play currently fall?

No one likes to end up on a plateau going nowhere with his or her game, but how many are willing to do something more to get off that plateau? Players willing to put forth the extra effort by taking lessons, studying or reading available instructional materials, or taking to the practice court to drill a problem area are usually not the ones whose games regress. They understand the work ethic that "you won't get something for nothing" and are willing to put forth the effort in search of something more from their games.

Better doubles play is a seemingly impossible task to some, but an exciting challenge to others. It depends a great deal on the *image* players have of themselves, the *belief* they have in themselves, and the level of *motivation* and *desire* they have to improve their games.

They way you see yourself depends on how you think of yourself. Positive thoughts must be used to form positive impressions, replacing any negative thoughts which might be present. Belief in yourself and your game will develop through practice and experience. This is why drilling and repetitive stroking in practice are so important. Your level of motivation and desire depends on how internally driven you are to excel. With very few exceptions, outside influences may motivate you temporarily but for any lasting motivational period it must come from within.

Do you *deserve* to be playing better? Have you put in the time, work, and effort to build your image and improve your game? Have you trained mentally and physically to develop confidence in yourself? If you haven't, not only will your game see marginal improvement, but you'll also be missing all the fun! It's not the end results that bring as much joy as expected, but rather it's the *challenge* along the way! Successful people have for centuries attested to the fact that it wasn't reaching the top that brought them the most joy but the journey there.

It is often the most difficult things in life that are the most rewarding. Push yourself and your game to new heights. Challenge yourself to better doubles play and you will discover more enjoyment while advancing. It's when the zest for the challenge is lost that your game begins to flounder. Remember, the rewards will come in the *quest,* so stop searching for them only at the end of the journey. Keep your game in a constant state of improvement and you're destined to continue traveling on the road to success!

⚲ SHARING AN EXPERIENCE WITH OTHERS

The social aspect of the game of doubles is what attracts many to the sport. Doubles offers an excellent opportunity for players to meet, compete, and have fun doing something together. It is a chance to share in an experience with friends, spouses, and others in a social environment playing a sport you enjoy.

This is not a "sales pitch" attempt to better promote doubles play, rather it's a reminder of the many benefits and reasons you should be playing the game of doubles. When you

Stan Smith and Bob Lutz sharing one of their many great moments in the sport.

find yourself feeling "flat" over your play, the quickest way to recover and get yourself playing well is once again to *enjoy playing the game.*

Relax and savor the time shared with others on the doubles court. Your play will be enhanced while you enjoy the game more through your positive emotions. It sounds simple: "Enjoy playing the game more and you'll play better," but that is how you can use positive thinking to your advantage. By fostering positive emotions and thoughts anything will be possible through your play and without your control over them, few things will be. Don't allow yourself to lose your "gusto" for this game, keep your excitement and joy in playing it and your chances for better play are certain to increase.

⚲ EXPERIMENT . . . IT'S FUN

Ever feel stagnant, uninspired, or unmotivated with your doubles game? Don't worry, it's happened to every player in the game at least once in their tennis life. When this happens you can let your game slump in the dullness created, or you can look for ways to escape from such sluggishness. A *change* is usually what is needed. A way to experience something new or different to bring excitement and fun back into your play.

Some players just need to break from the sport to rekindle their enthusiasm for playing. Too much tennis often brings staleness. The professional tour players are prime examples. They travel the world playing and practicing day in and day out whether they want to or not. When their desire slips so does their enthusiasm and playing level. This is why they often seek solace through vacations away from the sport.

Boredom is known to set in with players who are experiencing little improvement. They are in a routine and feel as though they are only going through the motions as they play. If this ever happens with your game, *search for a better understanding* of how to come out of it. It might be a *strategic* understanding that you are lacking or it might be a *mechanical* one. You will be able to continue on the road to improvement as long as you understand what it is that is keeping your game from advancing. Once the necessary understanding has been acquired, your rate of improvement will then depend on your level of discipline and determination.

There are limitless tactics, strategies, shots, and styles to use in playing the game of doubles. If your play is feeling old or mundane, *get creative!* Experiment with your play, it can be fun. The best time for this is usually during practice and social match play. Avoid such creative play during crucial matches unless you and your partner agree that this is the right time to implement the change.

Expand your thoughts on the game of doubles. Get a charge out of learning something new about your play. Make a partner switch or side change if necessary. Evaluate and change your goals if need be. Do something different — enter a tournament or a new league; create more excitement in your practices. Develop a new stroke or style of play. This game has far too much to offer its participants to ever let yourself get bored and not enjoy playing it!

♀ DOUBLES IS LIKE LIFE — IT'S WHAT YOU MAKE OF IT

Tennis crazies can easily forget that doubles is "just a game." They often are so immersed in playing the sport that it becomes such an important part of their lives. Although this in itself is not bad, if these same players are not careful, they might find themselves losing all perspective and making tennis seem more important than it really is. When this occurs, playing levels don't increase as many might think, rather they decrease since emotional control can be lost.

I've seen tennis control entire personalities in players. When they're playing well they are upbeat, friendly, and personable people. However, when these same players discover their games are off, they become moody, testy, and miserable souls, sometimes for days. It is important to put tennis in its proper perspective. Some days may require you simply to *laugh* at your on-court performances, but that can be the best way to remain in control of yourself and your emotions. Players who let their games affect their personalities are not in control of themselves. They will lower their playing level by distorting the importance of tennis in their lives.

Avoid placing unnecessary emphasis and pressure on yourself to perform. You will play up to your highest standards when *you're having fun and enjoying yourself on the court.* Remember, you will enjoy playing the game of doubles if you want to, and you probably won't enjoy it if you don't. The reason lies in your *attitude.* Only you are in control of it, no one else. If you don't learn to control it, you might find other influences, like the game of tennis, controlling you.

℺ YOU'LL ALL BE FRIENDS TOMORROW

I grew up playing tennis competitively. Players on the other side of the net were the "enemy" to me. Over time I learned to vent my view more toward myself and away from my opponents. Although I continued to look for weaknesses in my opponents and ways to exploit them, I became more concerned with optimum play in myself than beating those across the net.

Competitive doubles can be a real battle. Players try to score using tactics and strategies designed to pick opponents apart and make them look bad in the process. Emotions can be heated when tensions fill the air. Looks or even words can be exchanged. Pressures mount as each key point is played.

Some of the best performances ever recorded in sporting events around the world occurred when all the pressure was on. Competition offers players a chance at realizing their potential. It also, however, has been known to bring out the worst in some players.

Whatever your reason for playing the game of doubles, the social aspects, exercise, or personal betterment, you will always attain more enjoyment from this game through *positive thoughts and actions*. Learn to control your thoughts and actions on court whatever the situation. Show a little integrity and class and you will surely feel better about yourself, win more friends in life, and win more of the doubles matches you play as well!

℺ SUMMARY

Search to discover the reasons you enjoy playing the game of doubles. If regularly playing your best is what you're after, prepare yourself for it to happen. Don't expect it to happen on its own and be frustrated when it doesn't. Make your play more exciting by challenging yourself to improve. If you deserve to play well, you probably will. Don't avoid putting in the time and effort to develop your mental and physical state. You'll miss out on all the fun if you do! To raise your game from the "dead," start by enjoying it once again. Avoid falling into a slump by creating new and different twists to your practices and play. If you want to play consistently at your highest level you must remember to have *fun* and *enjoy your play.* It sounds simple, but by keeping your emotions positive, you'll be able to realize your best play . . . and do so on a more regular basis!

ℚ *ABOUT THE AUTHOR*

Skip Singleton is the Director of Tennis at Bluewater Bay Resort in Niceville, Florida. Bluewater Bay was selected by the Florida Tennis Association as "Tennis Club of the Year" for 1986-87 and 1988-89 and is a Five Star Rated Tennis Resort by *World Tennis Magazine*. Skip has received the highest rating of certified teaching professionals by the United States Professional Tennis Association and was named "Professional of the Year" by the USPTA Florida Division for 1989. He has held state and national rankings since he was a junior and has competed on professional circuits in the U.S. and Europe. He has worked both on and off the court with internationally known and respected coaches and players. Skip is involved in many aspects of the tennis industry and is currently an officer on the USPTA Florida Board, tournament director for the largest professional tennis event in northwest Florida, an active speaker nationally, and member of the Prince Teaching Professional Advisory Staff. Skip lives with his wife, Debbie, and dogs, Ace and Volley, at Bluewater Bay Resort in Niceville, Florida.

♀ ABOUT ROD LAVER

Red haired southpaw Rod Laver's list of tennis accomplishments is legend. "Rocket" is the only player to have twice won the Grand Slam of Tennis, winning Wimbledon, and the U.S., Australian and French Opens all the same year. Besides achieving this astonishing feat in 1962 and 1969, Laver also won two additional singles titles at Wimbledon and one more at the Australian Open. He won ten or twelve matches for Australia in Davis Cup Finals. Laver also chalked up an impressive doubles and mixed doubles record as well as winning nine Grand Slam doubles titles during his illustrious career. Born August 9, 1938 in Rockhampton, Queensland, Laver was the first tennis player in history to earn $1 million in prize money. Known for his powerful serve and "rocket-like" topspin forehand, Rod now resides in Newport Beach, California.

♉ *ABOUT LEROY NEIMAN*

LeRoy Neiman's art chronicles man at his leisure, not only sporting events, but Las Vegas, Fashion, the Opera, the Theater, Bars, Cars, and Resorts. All that glitters in present day American culture is colorfully rendered by Neiman's brush and pen. He is a superb draftsman and in addition, a brilliant colorist. Yet his art transcends his technical skill. He catches the moment and mood that is the essence of an event or happening. And his art seldom fails to evoke a response in the viewer such as — yes, that picture is the embodiment of the expectancy, color, and excitement of a critical point in a tennis match.

Index

A

Achieving consistent results, 71-80
Adjusting serving and receiving positions (illus.), 66
Adjusting your positions, 63-7
Admiring your own shot while the ball is still in play (Don't!), 87
Advancing through the levels, 115-127
Aerobic exercises, 125-6
Alley shot, 111
Analyzing team strengths and weaknesses, 21-3
Analyzing your opponents' weaknesses, 120-1
Analyzing your play, important after wins *and* losses, 118
Angles, 51, 52
  (illus.), 51
  understanding, 52
    as means of controlling play, 52
Arguments (team), how to settle, 135-6
Australian doubles, 69
Australian doubles formation, 68, 124
  (illus.), 68
Automatic poaching times, 106-7
"Automatic tennis", 44
Awareness, 41-2

B

Backward mobility, importance of, 91
Balancing the court 55, 62
  (illus.), 62
Ball control, 38-9, 124
  as part of total game, 124
  contact point, 38
  elements of, 38

follow-through, 38-9
footwork, 38
"freeze" analyses, 39
grip, 38
placement, 39
racket preparation, 38
Basic doubles, 71-2, 79-80
Basic strokes; serve, volley, overhead, return, lob, 122
Becoming "boring" champions, 79
Believing in yourself, 40-1
Better server serves first!, 71
Breaking your opponent's serve, 122

C

Category levels, 115-6
Changing a losing game, 72
"Check step", 83-5
  importance of timing, 83
  moving toward the ball, 85
Chip shot, 14
Commands, 31
Communication, 25-6, 32-3, 99-100, 135
  between partners, 25
  importance of, 25-6, 135
  importance of practicing, 32
  importance of with lobs, 99-100
  means of building confidence, 32-3
Compatible goals, importance of, 115-6
Competitive doubles, 145
Concentration, importance of, 16, 37, 74, 119-120
Consistent habits, importance of, 78-9
Contact point, 38
Control, 35-6, 42-3, 44
  of frustration with your partner, 44

(Control, continued)
of "nuisance" conditions, 35-6
of opponents, 35
of self, 35
of the match, 35
of your opponents, 42-3
Control of the game, 35
Control the net, control the point, 103
Controlled thinking, 37
Controlling the point, 89
"Court hog", 17
Creative doubles, 69-70
changing strategies, 69
Crosscourt shot, 111

D
Defensive lob, 94-5
Developing as a team, 21-34
Diplomacy, importance of to doubles
team, 26-8
Discipline, 35
Divorce Court Doubles, 129-137
Double the fun, 139-146
Doubles, 13-4, 16-7, 141-2, 143, 144, 145-6
a team sport, 13-4
as a social sport, 13, 141
greater variety of strokes, 14
just a game, 144
meant to be enjoyable, 143
social aspects of, 141-2
teamwork, 16-7
understand why you play, 145-6
why play?, 139
Double(s) trouble, 91-102
Doubles Difference, 13-20
Doubles diplomacy, 26-8
Doubles players, personality
characteristics, 16-7
Drop-volley, 14

E
Ego factor in doubles play, 134
Errors, unforced, 74

F
Facial expressions, importance of
controlling, 26
Fakes and double fakes, at the net, 107-8

First serve, 121
First serves, importance of, 72-3
Flach, Ken and Robert Seguso (photo),
54
Fleming, Peter and John McEnroe
(photo), 84, 92
Focus, 36-7
importance of sustaining, 37
Focusing your mind, 36-7
Follow-through, 38-9
Footwork, 38
"Frozen Delight", 112
Frustration with your partner, how to
control, 44

G
Going to the ball, 85-6
Great doubles teams, characteristics of,
19
Grip (racket), 38

H
Half-volley, 14
"Hit and see" tennis, 36
Hitting with purpose, 73-4
Hot/cold play, how to avoid, 76-7
Human relations skills, importance of,
26-7
Husband and wife teams, 130-1
on- and off-court feuding, 131
trading sides, 131

I
"I Formation", 61, 64 (illus.)
"In the zone", playing in, 40-1
Intelligent Tennis, 9
Intensity, increasing level of, 87-8, 90
body cues to notice, 88
International Racquet Sports
Association, 116
It takes two to win . . . or lose, 32-3

L
Laver, Rod, 148
Learning from your mistakes, 42
"Let it bounce!", 31
Letting your partner down, fear of, 40
Levels of play, 115-6

Listening, importance of, 26
Lloyd, John and Wendy Turnbull (photo), 56
Lob, 14, 72, 91, 93-5, 97-8, 99-100,
   best defense against aggressive play, 72
   communication problems, 99-100
   defeating with a good overhead, 97-8
   defensive, 94-5
   how to control, 93
   how to disguise, 93-4
   how to read, 98
   most effective shot in doubles, 93
   offensive, 94-5
   playing without a bounce, 99
   positioning problems, 100
   threat of the, 91
   return, 94
   volley, 94
Lobs and overheads; the shots that separate levels of doubles players, 100-101
Losing, should be a learning experience, 117-9
Luck, creating your own, 124-5
Lutz, Bob and Stan Smith (photo), 53, 142

M
"Marriage" of doubles partners, 28-9, 33-4
   good communications essential, 29
   importance of diplomacy, 33-4
   ingredients for success, 28-9
"Marriage counselor" (local professional), visiting a, 133-4
McEnroe, John and Peter Fleming (photo), 84, 92
Mental edge, 119-121
Mental requirements, 119-121
   acting — not reacting, 119-120
   importance of concentration, 119-120
   increase as level of play rises, 119
   strategic and tactical planning, 120-1
Mental toughness, 36, 39
Midcourt advantage, the, 81-90
"Mine!", 29
Mistakes, learning from your, 42

Mixed doubles, 129-130
   husband and wife teams, 130
   importance of positive thinking, 130
   instilling and restoring confidence, 129-130
   mental pressures, 129
"Moonballers", 93
Most effective shot in doubles, 93
Movement of players, 15
Movers, Poachers, and Shakers, 103-113
Moving together, 55
   the imaginary rope, 55
Moving with the ball, 96
   (illus.), 58
Moving with your partner (illus.), 59, 60

N
National Tennis Rating Program (NTRP), 116-7
Navratilova, Martina and Pam Shriver (photo), 22, 24
Neiman, LeRoy, 149
Net play, 47-8, 50, 75, 86-7, 107-110, 112
   crazy behavior works!, 108-9
   fakes and double fakes, 107-8
   gaining advantage, 48
   how to intimidate and confuse, 107-8
   importance of constant readiness, 109-110
   importance of positioning, 75
   keep moving, 112
   overcoming fear of the net, 47
   play as though every ball is coming to you, 109-110
   singles vs. doubles (illus.), 50
   stop and go movements, 86-7
   the intimidation factor, 48
   when your partner is serving, 112
Newcombe, John (photo), 82
"No Person's Land" (between midcourt and baseline), 89
NTRP (National Tennis Rating Program), 116-7
   rating categories, 116-7, 126

O
"Off" days, accepting in your partner, 27
Offensive lob, 94-5

One step rule (illus.), 49
Opponent evaluations, 23
Opponents, 42-3
    control of, 42-3
    exploiting their weaknesses, 43
    forcing them to follow your game
        plan, 43
Opponents' weaknesses, importance of
    analyzing, 120-1
Opportunistic waiting, 78
Overhead, 91, 95-9, 101-102
    deep to deep placements, 98-9
    importance of good footwork, 97
    importance of the three P's, 101-102
    maintaining ball control, 98-9
    need for a good stroke, 97-8
    need to practice, 91
    practice builds confidence, 97-8
    preparation for, 96-7
    short to short placements, 98-9
Overhead problems, 95-7
    "Pat and Mike" (your feet), 95-6
    poor footwork, 96
Overplaying the ball, 74

P
Parallel play, importance of, 55
Partner, 19-20
    importance of compatibility, 19
    need for complementary skills, 19-20
"Pat and Mike" (your feet), 95-6
Patience, importance of, 78-83
Percentage shots, importance of, 83
Personality characteristics of doubles
    players, 16-7
Placement, 39
Placing the ball, 73-4
Playing as one, 31-2
Playing in "automatic", 40-1
Playing the difficult teams, importance
    of, 119
Playing the game in control, 35-45
Playing the percentages, 71-2
Playing to your opponents' weaknesses,
    73
Poaching, 25, 103, 103-7
    "automatic" opportunities, 106-7
    importance of anticipation, 105-6

perfecting your timing, 106
    reading your opponents, 105-6
    strategies that work, 103-5
Poor play, fear of, 40
Positioning for success, 47-70
Positive thinking, 39-40
Positive thinking (you play as well as
    you think can), 121
Potential, reaching your, 140
Pressuring your opponents, 89
Proper positioning, 63-7
    net, 67
    receiving serve, 67
Put-aways, 75

R
Racket preparation, 38
Reading the ball, 61
Reissen, Marty and Sherwood Stewart
    (photo), 30
Reliable strokes, 72-3
Repetitive practice, 124-5
    importance of, 124-5
    with a purpose, 125
Return of serve, 57, 72-3
    (illus.), 57
Right partner, searching for, 18-9

S
Second serve, 121
Seguso, Robert and Ken Flach (photo),
    54
Self-confidence, 40-1
    developing through practice, 41
Self-control, 35
Self-discipline, 35
Self-esteem, yours and your partner's,
    33
Serve, 57, 72-3, 81, 99, 121-2, 125, 127
    breaking your opponent's, 122, 127
    first; must reach high percentage, 121
    holding takes team effort, 122
    how to improve, 125
    importance of varying, 121-2
    must hold to win, 121-2, 127
    return of (illus.), 57
    second; must be reliable, 121
Set-up shots, importance of, 81, 99

Shot selection, 23, 123-4
  advance planning of, 73-4
Shot, calling it, 29-31
Shot, who makes it?, 29-31
Shriver, Pam and Martina Navratilova
    (photo), 22, 24
Signaling, as means of communication,
    25
Singleton, Skip, 147
"Sitters", 75
Smith, Stan and Bob Lutz (photo), 53,
    142
Social aspects of doubles, 141-3
Standard doubles position (illus.), 65
Stewart, Sherwood and Marty Reissen
    (photo), 30
Stove, Betty (photo) 104
Strategic and tactical planning, 120-1
Strategies, 16, 23, 77-8
  adaptable, 77-8
    importance of unpredictability, 77
  team, 23
Strengths (yours) and weaknesses (your
    opponents), 41
Strokes, 121, 122
  basic: serve, volley, overhead, return,
    lob, 122
  consistency needed, 121
"Switch!", 31
Switching partners, 132

T
Talbert, Bill, 13
Team differences, 133
Team play, 14, 55
  playing as one, 31-2
Team strategies, 23
Team strengths and weaknesses, 22-3
Team, developing as a, 21-34

Teamwork, 16-7
Thoughts, controlling your, 39-40
Total game, 123-6
  better ball control, 124
  commitment to improving, 124
  elements of, 123-4
  importance of staying in shape, 125-6
  needed to advance, 123-4
  variety of strategic plans, 123-4
Trading sides, 131
Trial separation, 133
Tricks, developing a bag of, 122-3
Turnbull, Wendy and John Lloyd
    (photo), 56

U
Unforced errors, 74
United States Professional Tennis
    Association, 147
United States Tennis Association, 116
Unsportsmanlike conduct, 35

V
Volley, 14, 47-8
  offensive/defensive rule, 110-1
  positioning and footwork, 48
  successful, 86

W
Weaknesses, spotting in opponents, 41-2
Well-rounded game, importance of, 101
Who makes the shot?, 29-31
Winning habits, 78-9
Winning, not as important as learning
    and improving, 117-9
Working WITH your partner, 32

Y
"Yours!", 31

Skip Singleton's
INTELLIGENT TENNIS CAMP & CLINICS
at Bluewater Bay

For more information about Skip Singleton's INTELLIGENT TENNIS
CAMP & CLINICS write to:

> Skip Singleton, Director of Tennis
> Bluewater Bay
> P.O. Box 247
> Niceville, FL 32578